Y0-BNY-863

Perspectives in Churchmanship

Essays in Honor of Robert G. Torbet

edited by
David M. Scholer

MERCER
UNIVERSITY PRESS

ISBN 0-86554-268-6

CONTENTS

EDITORIAL INTRODUCTION

This is the third *Festschrift* to appear as an issue of *Perspectives in Religious Studies*. The first two honored Southern Baptist scholars; this issue honors one of the "giants" of American Baptist scholar-churchmen. It is a great honor and joy, on behalf of the National Association of Baptist Professors of Religion, to edit this volume as a tribute to Robert G. Torbet and his many lasting accomplishments and influences. Torbet is probably best known for his contributions to Baptist history, identity, denominational structure and ecumenical concerns. Thus, the following articles attempt to address these particular issues.

A biographical article on Robert G. Torbet is provided by Norman H. Maring, Emeritus Professor of Church History, Eastern Baptist Theological Seminary, where he taught for 36 years. Maring, honored by a *Festschrift* issue of the *American Baptist Quarterly* in June 1985, has known and worked with Torbet for over 40 years. Maring is probably best known for his *A Baptist Manual of Polity and Practice* (1963; 1981) authored with Winthrop S. Hudson.

The bibliography of Torbet's publications was prepared by Jane Millikan, an American Baptist Master of Divinity senior at Northern Baptist Theological Seminary, who is also my Student Assistant.

Robert T. Handy, Henry Sloane Coffin Professor of Church History, Emeritus, Union Theological Seminary (New York), has offered a study of religious freedom and its place in Baptist identity and history. Handy is author and editor of at least 10 books on American or Baptist religious history and life, including *A Christian America: Protestant Hopes and Historical Realities* (2d ed., 1984); *A History of the Churches in the United States and Canada* (1976) and *The Social Gospel in America* (1966).

Stanley J. Grenz, Associate Professor of Systematic Theology and Christian Ethics, North American Baptist Seminary, writes out of the context of his 1983 book *Isaac Backus—Puritan and Baptist* . . . Grenz has also authored *The Baptist Congregation: A Guide to Baptist Belief and Practice* (1985).

Samuel S. Hill, Professor of Religion, University of Florida, co-authored with Torbet in 1964 *Baptists—North and South*. Hill here takes up again his interests in "Southern religion," reflected also in his various books such as *Southern Churches in Crisis* (1967), *Religion and the Solid South* (1972), *South and North in American Religion* (1980) and *Religion in the Southern States* (1983).

William H. Brackney, formerly Executive Director of the American Baptist Historical Society and now Dean of Eastern Baptist Theological Seminary, addresses the issue of Baptist identity directly. Brackney has edited *Baptist Life and Thought, 1600-1980: A Source Book* (1983).

Eric H. Ohlmann, Professor of Christian Heritage and Associate Dean, Northern Baptist Theological Seminary, has also offered a study in the area of Baptist identity. Ohlmann, a Canadian, has taught at Northern Baptist for over 15 years, including regular courses on Baptist thought and Baptist history.

The brief outline reflection on the World Council of Churches' *Baptism, Eucharist and Ministry* is my summary of a discussion of this document by the Faculty of Northern Baptist Theological Seminary, which took place as part of that institution's own process of attempting to define Baptist identity.

Walter B. Shurden, Callaway Professor of Christianity, Mercer University, provides a historical study closely related to the theme of Torbet's first book and to his continuing interests in Baptist ecclesiastical structure. Shurden has authored *Not a Silent People: Controversies That Have Shaped Southern Baptists* (1972), *Associationalism among Baptists in America, 1707-1814* (1980) and *The Life of Baptists in the Life of the World: 80 Years of the Baptist World Alliance (1985)*.

It is my hope and that of the National Association of Baptist Professors of Religion that, as the life and work of Robert G. Torbet already has, these essays honoring him will contribute to the enrichment and strengthening of Baptist life and its contributions to the whole Church of Jesus Christ.

David M. Scholer

David M. Scholer is Dean of the Seminary and Julius R. Mantey Professor of New Testament, Northern Baptist Theological Seminary, Lombard, Illinois.

ROBERT G. TORBET: SCHOLAR-TEACHER AND CHURCHMAN

NORMAN H. MARING
EASTERN BAPTIST THEOLOGICAL SEMINARY (EMERITUS)
PHILADELPHIA PA 19151

If one wishes a word to characterize the ways in which Robert Torbet has lived out his Christian calling, that of ''Churchman'' seems most appropriate. Hundreds of former students will attest his scholarship and contributions as a teacher, and others will witness to his abilities as an administrator. In all of these employments, as well as in his position as the Ecumenical Officer for the American Baptist Churches, USA, he has been motivated by a deep devotion to Jesus Christ and his Church. Robert C. Campbell, General Secretary of that denomination, has stated: ''As a denominational leader, Robert has probably done more than any other person to enrich the ecumenical outlook of the American Baptist Churches. His responsiveness and sensitivity to all American Baptists, combined with his historical, biblical, and theological expertise, have brought multitudes of American Baptists into the ecumenical stream.''

Born in Spokane, Washington, Robert George Torbet soon moved to St. Paul, Minnesota, where he grew up. In 1930, he entered Wheaton (IL) College, where he was elected to the Honor Society. Following graduation, he matriculated at the Eastern Baptist Theological Seminary, in Philadelphia, a school then in its tenth year of existence.

As a member of the seminary faculty in those days, L. Sarle Brown, recalls, the administration and faculty early recognized his exceptional talents and engaged him as a part-time instructor in Literature in the fledgling Collegiate Department of the Seminary. In his second year he began graduate study at the University of Pennsylvania, being the recipient of one of the prized scholarships awarded annually. The requirements for the M.A. degree in history were satisfied in 1937, the same year in which he received the B.D. degree from the Seminary.

Upon graduating from Penn and the Seminary, he was appointed a full-time Instructor of Literature and History in the Collegiate Department of the Seminary; and the following year received the title of Professor of these subjects. This Collegiate Department was in process of being expanded from a two-year program to a four-year college course leading to the A.B. degree. It was not open to the general public, but was exclusively for persons preparing for the Gospel ministry. Perceptive, methodical, and hard-working, Robert Torbet was the soul of efficiency, impressing colleagues and students with the prodigious amount of work which he could accomplish. For the next seven years he carried a full teaching load, with all of its concomitant duties, frequently preached on Sundays, and pursued graduate work at the University of Pennsylvania, where he received the Ph.D. degree in History in 1944.

A contemporary and long-time faculty colleague, Culbert G. Rutenber, offers an interesting sidelight. Always well-organized and prompt in meeting engagements or deadlines, Torbet had the enviable trait of leaving the office after a day's work with a clean desktop. Rutenber, or "Cubby" as he was familiarly known even to students, was much less systematic; and his desk was always cluttered with piles of books, letters, and papers, causing people to wonder how he ever knew where to find anything. On one occasion Torbet was in his office and expressed his annoyance at the disarray on the desk. "Cubby," he exclaimed, "if you would keep things more orderly, you would be able to think better!" Subsequently, Rutenber was appointed by the administration to be co-editor with Robert on an alumni publication, *The Easterner*. As he recalls, Torbet was exasperated with his lack of organization and asked him just to look after the mailings, and "finally he couldn't stand the way I operated and took over the whole thing." Both of these men had exceptional intellectual gifts and made outstanding contributions, but their styles differed as night from day.

Although he was serious, almost austere, in formal academic relationships, there was another side to him. Sometimes in the evening, when he had put his work aside, he might telephone over to the seminary to invite two or three students to his home for a cup of tea, and for an hour or so they would chat, listen to music, or perhaps play some table game. Those who had the opportunity to see him in such a context knew that he was a genial and warm human being. One former student, William F. Keucher, who subsequently became a denominational leader and President of Central Baptist Theological Seminary, recalls that in informal relationships, "I saw another side to this disciplined scholar. Sunny and warm, he had and has a deep care for persons. Beneath everything, there is a shepherd's pastoral heart.''

Another student from those early days, L. Doward McBain, says that in his first year in the pre-theological department he was discouraged and ready to quit; but ''Dr. Torbet sensed that something was wrong. He invited me to his apartment, then asked me to look back on my life and see how far I had come.'' As a result of this conversation and some further encouragement, he was able to put things in clearer perspective. ''My faith was restored,'' he reports; and he is grateful for the kind attention which led him to finish college and seminary. Later he was to become a prominent pastor and preacher, and eventually President of the American Baptist Seminary of the West.

Many men and women who studied with Dr. Torbet in the Collegiate Department of the Seminary, and in the Seminary itself, have looked back in later years to thank him for his heartening words and for aiding them to develop abilities to express ideas in writing and speech. Many have been indebted to him for having introduced them to good literature and a lively use of the imagination, as well as for an appreciation of the importance of historical studies. He also served as a model of disciplined thinking, careful time management, and diligence in work. Torbet organized and sponsored for several years a Literary Society, the Elthonians, in which many learned the arts of public speaking, argumentation, and parliamentary procedure.

The generous spirit of helpfulness was not limited to students, but was expressed in other associations. In all of the positions he held he has been known for sensitivity to the needs of others. In many instances he has gone out of his way to assist graduate students with advice on research, persons seeking employment in higher education, and pastors or laypersons who have asked for counsel. I remember, for example, hearing a colleague, D. George Vanderlip, speak of Dr. Torbet's instrumentality in aiding him to find his first teaching position. As he neared the end of his doctoral program, he had made some inquiries about possible placement only to receive discouraging replies. At a chance meeting with Dr. Torbet, he had told him of his aspiration to teach in a theological seminary and found a sympathetic ear. Torbet offered helpful suggestions which resulted in Vanderlip's finding a position in a Baptist seminary the next fall. The same spirit of willingness to be helpful has continued in retirement. Just a few months ago a new professor in a Southern Baptist seminary told me of the warm welcome he received when he asked to talk with Torbet about a book in progress. He received not only warm hospitality, but useful advice which had a part in the recent publication of his book. Illustrations of this kind might be multiplied, as they are typical of Robert Torbet's concern for people.

Having taught courses in general history and literature for seven years, and having earned his Ph.D., Torbet became the Professor of Church History at Eastern Baptist Seminary, in 1944. At Penn his graduate work had been in British and American history, where he benefited from the tutelage of some of the outstanding contemporary scholars, such as Conyers Read, Richard Shryock, and Roy Nichols. This broad acquaintance with history, along with courses in Church History taken in seminary, laid an excellent foundation for teaching courses in the history of the Christian Church.

A special interest in Baptist history had already begun to develop, as he wrote his doctoral dissertation on *A Social History of the Philadelphia Baptist Association*. Published in 1944, this volume explored new territory, and it manifested the kind of painstaking research in primary sources which were to characterize so much of his later writing. It constituted an important contribution in a field which was fairly new and still in process of being defined.

In 1944, there were many periods of Church History for which there was a dearth of suitable textbooks. A new surge of interest in religious studies was on the horizon, particularly with the emergence of social and intellectual history and an appreciation of the significant role of religion in the development of American character and institutions. The following two decades saw the institution of departments of religion in universities, and this fact also contributed to the production of monographs and surveys for use by students. At this earlier stage, however, there was a lack of good textbooks in general Church History and in Baptist History.

In a Baptist seminary, where a course in the history of Baptists was a requirement for all students, the lack of a textbook in the field was very obvious to Dr. Torbet as he began to teach courses in this field. Characteristically, he soon set to work to remedy the situation, as he began to gather materials for a book. In 1950, *A History of the Baptists* appeared. The challenge presented by this task is not so easy to appreciate today, when there are many more monographs and studies to use as building blocks for a general survey. It was intended to provide a comprehensive survey of Baptists all over the world, but devoted major attention to Baptists of the United States, where of course they are by far the most numerous.

As the late Dr. Kenneth Scott Latourette, noted historian of Christian Missions, at Yale, and a prominent Baptist, wrote in the ''Foreword'': ''A great need exists for a fresh account of what has been done earlier, and which will give a comprehensive view of the entire course of Baptist history and bring it down to date. . . . This Professor Torbet has done. What he has here given us represents years of reading and patient research. Nowhere else is there to be found in so nearly inclusive and up-to-date fashion a summary of the people who bear the name of Baptist.''

The book filled a void and found welcome reception as it began to be used in college and seminary courses in both the North and the South. Revised from time to time, the book has seen changes in interpretations to reflect new, scholarly research, the addition of new information and the up-dating of bibliographical resources. It has gone through ten printings. A measure of the difficulty of producing such a comprehensive volume is the fact that no one to date has written a similar book to become a competitor. At the same time, for laypersons he revised a book by Henry K. Rowe, *The Baptist Witness* (1951).

Just as Dr. Torbet was becoming widely recognized as a Baptist historian and teacher, he accepted a new position as an editor with the American Baptist Board of Education and Publication. An experienced writer, broadly educated, and accustomed to work which required meticulous attention to details, he was well qualified for an editorial post. Indeed, for nearly ten years he had edited an alumni publication at the Seminary, called *The Easterner*. At the request of the Seminary administration, he had accepted responsibility for the new venture in 1942, almost single-handedly planning and preparing for publication this periodical containing articles, book reviews, and alumni news each month for nearly a decade. The new position made him responsible for a wider range of publications, and he had more assistance, but the procedures were familiar already. After four years in this post, he was asked to become the Director of Educational Services. At a time when colleges and universities were flourishing, and many Baptists, as well as others, were in graduate schools looking forward to teaching in higher education, there was a need for help in locating teaching positions. There were also many Baptist students in need of financial aid to pursue their studies, and the new position was also designed to assist in locating funds. Torbet served in this post for three years until 1958.

The years with the Board of Education and Publication did not deter Dr. Torbet from his interest in research and writing. A major research project was undertaken at the instigation of the American Baptist Foreign Mission Societies, eventuating in the publication of *Venture of Faith: The Story of American Baptist Foreign Missions* (Judson Press, 1955). This comprehensive history of the work of the American Baptist Foreign Mission Societies from 1814 to 1954 was an outstanding achievement, much of it based upon original research in manuscript sources, correspondence, and records. That it was all done while he continued to work full-time at the ABEEP attests his ability to work diligently and efficiently.

There were also lesser publications in these years, more popular books written for study groups in churches. First came *The Baptist Ministry*: *Then and Now*, published in 1953. Next came *The Baptist Story*, in 1957, offering a succinct account of Baptist life and thought for those not likely to read the longer volumes. In addition, numerous articles were contributed to encyclopedias and periodicals. Thus, even though he was not directly involved in theological education, his reputation as a Baptist scholar increased, and he was soon asked to join a theological faculty again.

In 1958, after some urging, he accepted an invitation to become the Dean and Professor of Church History at Central Baptist Theological Seminary in Kansas City, Kansas. Here was an opportunity to combine his talents for teaching and for administration. Once more his reputation was established as a teacher who was well informed, always punctual, always prepared, and expecting excellence in the performance of students. Here, too, as his successor, Fred E. Young, has observed, he showed a personal interest in students, always ready to talk with them about personal or academic problems, and making every effort to assist them in finding financial resources to enable them to continue their studies.

He came to Central at a critical time in its history. Founded just after the turn of the century in a border state, the seminary had drawn students from North and South. Southern Baptists had been in the student body, the faculty and the board of trustees; and southern churches had contributed to its support. In the 1950's, however, as Southern Baptists were becoming more expansive and unwilling to observe long-standing comity agreements, the cooperation with Central Baptist Seminary ended, and Southern Baptists established a new seminary, Midwestern, in Kansas City, Missouri. Although financially weakened by this development, Central's administration and faculty determined to move ahead with their intention to seek accreditation from the American Association of Theological Schools. To accomplish this goal, capable academic leadership was needed to strengthen faculty, library, and curriculum. In this situation, Dr. Torbet was able to assist the president and faculty in reordering the academic program to make it acceptable to the Association of Theological Schools.

In spite of the demands of his position as dean and professor of church history, he did not abandon writing. During his years at Central, he continued to write occasional articles and three books. First, came a biography, *Reuben E. Nelson: Free Churchman* (1961), written in collaboration with Henry R. Bowler. It recounted the life and contributions of the first General Secretary of the American Baptist Convention, who served from 1950 until his death in 1960. Next, came a survey of *The Protestant Reformation*, aimed at a popular readership and adapted for use in church study groups (1961). In 1964, as several of the Baptist church bodies in the United States contemplated a joint celebration of the 150th anniversary of the first American Baptist foreign missionary society, the Triennial Convention, there was interest in comparing Southern and Northern Baptists who had begun this mission venture together in 1814. Together with Samuel Hill, of the University of North Carolina, Dr. Torbet published *Baptists—North and South* (1964).

It was during his years at Central, too, that he was elected President of the American Baptist Convention (now called the American Baptist Churches, USA). An honorary position, the office of president requires a great deal of travel, endless committee meetings, many speaking engagements, and other kinds of assignments. It also offers opportunity to influence policies and directions which the denomination is to take. As one colleague notes: "As President of ABC/USA, he brought scholarship and service together as he led our denomination with clarity of vision and with steadfast conviction."

At the end of eight years at Central, the denomination once more co-opted him for a special task. The 1950s had provided a climate favorable to the development of Dr. Torbet's growing appreciation of the larger Church. Influenced by his study of church history, by publications of the early Faith and Order Conference, and by the writings of such British Baptists as Ernest A. Payne, H. Wheeler Robinson, and Henry Cook, as well as those of Willem A. Visser 't Hooft, Torbet had become greatly interested in the ecumenical movement. In 1954, he had represented the American Baptist Convention at the WCC Assembly in Evanston, Illinois; and in 1963, he became a representative of the denomination as observer-consultant in the meetings of COCU (Consultation on Church Union).

In a period when ecumenism was thus thriving and denominational mergers were being effected, there was a growing sentiment in favor of uniting several major denominations in the United States. Known as COCU, it began in 1962 with Episcopalians and United Presbyterians; before long they were joined by United Methodists and the United Church of Christ; soon others came aboard to share in the quest for a road which would lead to actual union. American Baptist Churches, like several other denominations, were not ready for full participation, but did not want to remain completely aloof. They were permitted to send observers to the COCU meetings. Dr. Torbet had been an observer for the American Baptists since 1963. As interest in merger waxed, a lively discussion arose within his denomination concerning a move to become full participants.

There were strong feelings in support of joining the Consultation, but an even larger group opposed such a step. It was decided by the General Council of the denomination that it would be unwise to enter more fully into the church union negotiations. Instead, it requested that the American Baptists be allowed to send observer-consultants, making it possible to contribute to the discussions as well as to observe. At the same time, it was decided that the American Baptist Churches ought to have a specific agency to represent them in ecumenical relations. Therefore, an Office of Ecumenical Relations was created, and Robert Torbet was appointed as the Assistant General Secretary for Ecumenical Relations. He entered upon his new duties at the beginning of 1967 and remained in this post until his retirement at the end of 1977.

With his broad background in church history, his knowledge of the Baptist heritage and doctrine, his ability to articulate his thoughts, he was well suited for the newly-created position. He represented the American Baptist Churches in many formal and informal gatherings, from the National and World Councils of Churches to consultations with Roman-Catholics and Jewish leaders. He served on the Executive Committee of the NCCC and the Central Committee of the WCC. He directed consultations between American Baptists and the Church of the Brethren and between the former and the Progressive National Baptist Convention, out of which came two special relationships. To keep American Baptists posted, a newsletter was begun which provided factual and interpretative data on ecumenical affairs. Tracts and booklets were written to inform constituents in the churches about the nature of the ecumenical movement, its biblical roots and its practical consequences. He spoke at countless gatherings, large and small, attempting to help people comprehend the importance of reaching more visible ways of achieving Christian unity. As a colleague in this enterprise has commented: ''Never compromising his convictions. . . . ever devoted to his Baptist heritage, he served as an exemplary statesman in the broader Church.'' Deeply concerned about Christian unity, he was nevertheless aware of the obstacles faced by Baptists and others when they contemplated any Church union or close ties with denominations which might minimize the importance of believer's baptism and which might insist upon an episcopal system of church government. To point up the wider problems faced by churches in the Free Church tradition, he wrote another book, *Ecumenism: Free Church Dilemma* (1968).

A strong interest in the Church at its many levels and its varied expressions has continued in retirement. Unexpected health problems have somewhat restricted his activities, but he has continued to live a fairly active life, being a faithful member of his home church, First Baptist Church of Philadelphia, and occasionally serving as a consultant for an agency of the denomination. Just recently, for example, he gave addresses to a conference of American Baptist Men on ''A Theology of Associations,'' emphasizing the necessity for Christian unity and cooperation within a denomination as well as between diverse communions. On another level, he is writing a book on Christian unity, *A Guide to the Understanding of the Twentieth-Century Ecumenical Movement*. Beginning with a description of the biblical-theological bases for Christian unity, it traces the history of Christian unity over the centuries, concentrating upon the present century.

In retirement Dr. Torbet continues to reside in the Philadelphia area. His interest in reading and music occupy much of his time, as he tries to keep abreast of Church affairs and with national and international trends. He is always glad to hear from a former student, colleague, or acquaintance, or to welcome those who drop by for a social visit. Although he is not given much to dwelling on the past, there are many achievements in which he can take satisfaction from his varied involvements in the life of the Church and the ways in which he has ordered his life in the attempt to serve the Lord Jesus Christ.

As one of those who is greatly indebted to Dr. Torbet as a teacher and as a friend for half a century, it is a pleasure to have a small share in this tribute honoring Robert Torbet for his years of service.

ROBERT G. TORBET:
A BIBLIOGRAPHY

JANE MILLIKAN
NORTHERN BAPTIST THEOLOGICAL SEMINARY
LOMBARD,IL

Robert G. Torbet's writings number over seventy items written during a period of more than forty years. This list is an attempt to be as complete as possible, although book reviews are not included. Entries are arranged alphabetically within each section.

I would especially like to thank Robert G. Torbet for providing extensive information for this bibliography. William Brackney, Executive Director, and Susan Eltscher, Director of the Library, of the American Baptist Historical Society were also very helpful.

BOOKS

Torbet, Robert G. *The Baptist Ministry: Then and Now*. Philadelphia: Judson, 1953.
_____. *The Baptist Story*. Valley Forge: Judson, 1957.
_____. *Ecumenism: Free Church Dilemma*. Valley Forge: Judson, 1968.
_____. *God's Word in Our Language*. Valley Forge: Judson, 1963.
_____. *A History of the Baptists*. Philadelphia: Judson, 1950; Second edition, Valley Forge: Judson, 1963; Third edition, Valley Forge: Judson, 1973.
_____. *The Protestant Reformation*. Valley Forge: Judson, 1961.
_____. *A Social History of the Philadelphia Baptist Association, 1707-1940*. Philadelphia: Westbrook, 1944.

_____. *Venture of Faith: A History of American Baptist Foreign Mission Society and the Woman's American Baptist Foreign Mission Society, 1814-1954.* Valley Forge: Judson, 1955.

JOINTLY AUTHORED BOOKS

Torbet, Robert G. *The Baptist Witness* (revision of *Baptists: Their Heritage and Purpose*, by Henry K. Rowe). Philadelphia: Judson, 1951.
_____. *Baptists—North and South* (with Samuel S. Hill, Jr.). Valley Forge: Judson, 1964.
_____. *Reuben E. Nelson: Free Churchman* (with Henry R. Bowler). Valley Forge: Judson, 1961.

ARTICLES

Torbet, Robert G. "American Baptist Churches in the USA," Chapter 6 in *Baptist Relations with Other Christians* (ed. James Leo Garrett; Valley Forge: Judson, 1974), 53-66.
_____. "American Baptist Churches USA," *The Brethren Encyclopedia*, Vol. 1 (ed. Donald F. Durnbaugh; Philadelphia: Brethren Encyclopedia, 1983), 22.
_____. "Amerikanische und Kanadische Baptisten," Chapter 13 in *Die Baptisten* (ed. John D. Hughey; Die Kirchen der Welt, Bd. 2; Stuttgart: Evangelisches Verlagswerk, 1964), 151-65.
_____. "The Association in Baptist Church Life," *Easterner* (November 1953).
_____. "Baptism—A Live Issue," *Baptist Leader* 19:10 (January 1958): 5,78.
_____. "Baptist Churches in America," Chapter 10 in *The American Church of the Protestant Heritage* (ed. Vergilius T. A. Ferm; New York: Philosophical Library, 1953), 187-206.
_____. "The Baptist Concept of the Church," *The Chronicle* 15 (1952): 3-18.
_____. "Baptist Contributions to Protestantism," *Baptist Leader* 9:4 (July 1947): 18-21.
_____. "The Baptist Ministry in Perspective," *Baptist Leader* 24:10 (January 1963): 8-9, 41.
_____. "Baptist Theological Education: An Historical Survey," *Foundations* 6 (1963): 311-35.
_____. "Baptist Thought About the Church," *Foundations* 1 (1958): 18-37.
_____. "The Baptist Witness," *Easterner* (January 1946).
_____. "Baptist World Alliance," *Twentieth Century Encyclopedia of Religious Knowledge* (ed. Lefferts A. Loetscher; Grand Rapids: Baker, 1955), 1:109.

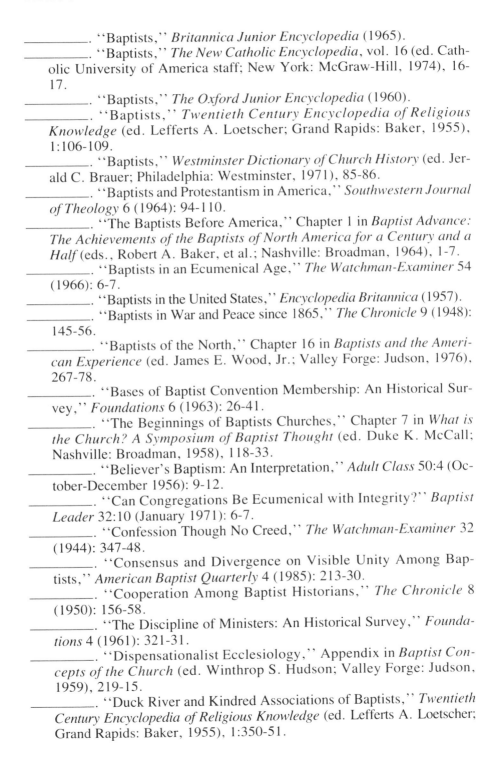

_____. "Baptists," *Britannica Junior Encyclopedia* (1965).

_____. "Baptists," *The New Catholic Encyclopedia*, vol. 16 (ed. Catholic University of America staff; New York: McGraw-Hill, 1974), 16-17.

_____. "Baptists," *The Oxford Junior Encyclopedia* (1960).

_____. "Baptists," *Twentieth Century Encyclopedia of Religious Knowledge* (ed. Lefferts A. Loetscher; Grand Rapids: Baker, 1955), 1:106-109.

_____. "Baptists," *Westminster Dictionary of Church History* (ed. Jerald C. Brauer; Philadelphia: Westminster, 1971), 85-86.

_____. "Baptists and Protestantism in America," *Southwestern Journal of Theology* 6 (1964): 94-110.

_____. "The Baptists Before America," Chapter 1 in *Baptist Advance: The Achievements of the Baptists of North America for a Century and a Half* (eds., Robert A. Baker, et al.; Nashville: Broadman, 1964), 1-7.

_____. "Baptists in an Ecumenical Age," *The Watchman-Examiner* 54 (1966): 6-7.

_____. "Baptists in the United States," *Encyclopedia Britannica* (1957).

_____. "Baptists in War and Peace since 1865," *The Chronicle* 9 (1948): 145-56.

_____. "Baptists of the North," Chapter 16 in *Baptists and the American Experience* (ed. James E. Wood, Jr.; Valley Forge: Judson, 1976), 267-78.

_____. "Bases of Baptist Convention Membership: An Historical Survey," *Foundations* 6 (1963): 26-41.

_____. "The Beginnings of Baptists Churches," Chapter 7 in *What is the Church? A Symposium of Baptist Thought* (ed. Duke K. McCall; Nashville: Broadman, 1958), 118-33.

_____. "Believer's Baptism: An Interpretation," *Adult Class* 50:4 (October-December 1956): 9-12.

_____. "Can Congregations Be Ecumenical with Integrity?" *Baptist Leader* 32:10 (January 1971): 6-7.

_____. "Confession Though No Creed," *The Watchman-Examiner* 32 (1944): 347-48.

_____. "Consensus and Divergence on Visible Unity Among Baptists," *American Baptist Quarterly* 4 (1985): 213-30.

_____. "Cooperation Among Baptist Historians," *The Chronicle* 8 (1950): 156-58.

_____. "The Discipline of Ministers: An Historical Survey," *Foundations* 4 (1961): 321-31.

_____. "Dispensationalist Ecclesiology," Appendix in *Baptist Concepts of the Church* (ed. Winthrop S. Hudson; Valley Forge: Judson, 1959), 219-15.

_____. "Duck River and Kindred Associations of Baptists," *Twentieth Century Encyclopedia of Religious Knowledge* (ed. Lefferts A. Loetscher; Grand Rapids: Baker, 1955), 1:350-51.

_____. "Expansion of Christianity (Ancient)," *Twentieth Century Encyclopedia of Religious Knowledge* (ed. Lefferts A. Loetscher; Grand Rapids: Baker, 1955), 1:410-12.

_____. "Hard-Shell Baptists," *Twentieth Century Encyclopedia of Religious Knowledge* (ed. Lefferts A. Loetscher; Grand Rapids: Baker, 1955), 1:490.

_____. "Heretics in Early Christianity," *Twentieth Century Encyclopedia of Religious Knowledge* (ed. Lefferts A. Loetscher; Grand Rapids: Baker, 1955), 1:503-504.

_____. "Heritage of Freedom: Contributions to Protestant Expansion," *Baptist Leader* 9:5 (1947): 13-16.

_____. "Historical Background of the Southern Baptist 'Invasion,' " *Crusader* 14:8 (September 1959): 6-7.

_____. "Historical Background of the Southern Baptist 'Invasion,' " *Foundations* 2:4 (October 1959): 314-19.

_____. "In What Sense Is the American Baptist Convention a Manifestation of the Church?" in *Consultation Concerning Theological Implications of American Baptist Convention Organization and Structure* (1964) [no continuous pagination].

_____. "In What Sense Is the American Baptist Convention a Manifestation of the Church?" *Foundations* 8 (1965): 117-31.

_____. "Landmarkism," Chapter 7 in *Baptist Concepts of the Church* (ed. Winthrop S. Hudson; Valley Forge: Judson 1959), 170-95.

_____. "Lessons Learned in the Ecumenical Movement," *The Watchman-Examiner* 56 (1968): 742-43.

_____. "The Lord's Supper: An Interpretation," *Adult Class* 51:1 (January-March 1957): 4-7, 12.

_____. "Makers of Christian History," *Baptist Leader* 10:7 (October 1948): 61-65.

_____. "The Meaning of Evanston," *Easterner* (November 1954).

_____. "The Nature and Communication of Grace," *Foundations* 12 (1969): 213-31.

_____. "Options for a Viable Baptist Church Order," *Foundations* 13 (1970): 237-47.

_____. "Pluralism and Religious Liberty," *Report from the Capital* 22:5 (July 1967): 5.

_____. "A Preamble to a Proposal for Restructure of the American Baptist Convention," in *The Final Report of the Study Commission on Denominational Structure of the American Baptist Convention* (1972), 99-104.

_____. "Religious Liberty and Religion in the Public Schools," *Foundations* 4 (1961): 4-17.

_____. "A Response to R. J. Thompson's Paper on 'New Style Elders—A Warning,' " *Baptist World Alliance Study Papers* (1976) (Washington, DC: Baptist World Alliance, 1976) [an unpaginated two page article].

_____. ''Scopes Trial,'' *Twentieth Century Encyclopedia of Religious Knowledge* (ed. Lefferts A. Loetscher; Grand Rapids: Baker, 1955), 2:1004.

_____. ''Some Questions Answered,'' *Baptist Leader* 20:1 (April 1958): 38.

_____. ''Ulfilas,'' *Twentieth Century Encyclopedia of Religious Knowledge* (ed. Lefferts A. Loetscher; Grand Rapids: Baker, 1955), 2:1129.

_____. ''United American Free-Will Baptists, Colored,'' *Twentieth Century Encyclopedia of Religious Knowledge* (ed. Lefferts A. Loetscher; Grand Rapids: Baker, 1955), 2:1134.

_____. ''The Whole Household of God,'' *Mission* 167:2 (February 1969).

_____. ''The Word of God: Inspired and Authoritative,'' *Easterner* (December 1949).

PAMPHLETS AND UNPUBLISHED PAPERS

These items, with the exception of those marked ''*,'' are found in the American Baptist Historical Society collection.

Torbet, Robert G. *''After 450 Years—A New Thing'' [A report on American Baptist-Roman Catholic dialogue between 1967-1972] (Valley Forge: Office of Ecumenical Relations of American Baptist Churches USA, n.d.).

_____. ''The American Baptist Convention's Attitudes toward and Relations with Other Christians'' (Commission on Cooperative Christianity, 1971).

_____. ''Baptist Leadership'' (Department of Evangelism, American Baptist Home Mission Society, 1954).

_____. ''Bases of Baptist Convention Membership: An Historical Survey'' (General Council, American Baptist Churches USA, 1962).

_____. ''Church History and Church Leadership'' (American Baptist Historical Society, 1959).

_____. ''Doors to Tomorrow'' (Christian Higher Education, 1966).

_____. ''La Esencia de Nuestro Testimonio'' (Convencion Nacional Bautista de Mexico, (1966).

_____. *''Guidelines for Baptists in Church Union Talks'' (American Baptist Foreign Mission Society, 1971).

_____. ''Landmarkism'' (National Theological Conference, 1959).

_____. ''Local Autonomy: A Baptist Dilemma'' (Associated Home Mission Agencies of the American Baptist Convention, 1966).

_____. ''The Nature of Church Membership'' (American Baptist Publication Society, 1957).

_____. ''Notes on the Association in Baptist Church Life'' (State Secretaries' Council, 1955).

_____. ''The Pastor and the Power Structure of the Convention'' (Chicago Baptist Association, 1967).

_____. ''The People Called Baptists'' (American Baptist Board of Education and Publishing, n.d.).

_____. ''Report to the General Council on the Consultation on Church Union'' (1965).

_____. ''Selected Readings on Landmarkism'' (n.d.).

_____. ''What Baptists Believe'' (Department of Evangelism, American Baptist Convention, 1951).

_____. ''What Should Be Our Relationship to Other Christians in the Larger Witness Today?'' (Detroit Association of American Baptist Churches, 1966).

THE PRINCIPLE OF RELIGIOUS FREEDOM AND THE DYNAMICS OF BAPTIST HISTORY[1]

ROBERT T. HANDY
UNION THEOLOGICAL SEMINARY (EMERITUS)
NEW YORK NY 10027

There are many Baptist congregations and conventions of great variety across the face of the earth; a recent count by the not fully inclusive Baptist World Alliance reports 127 conventions or unions serving 142 countries. When we try to explain why such a diverse flock can be identified as Baptist, we often resort to pointing to a list of Baptist principles which in a general way are shared by all. I've seen various lists of such principles, and along with such emphases as the lordship of Christ, the authority of Scripture, believers' baptism, and congregational polity, I always find religious freedom. Whatever interpretation of Baptist origins you find convincing, the principle of religious freedom will be stressed. It is one of the clear identifying marks of the people called Baptist.

The words "religious freedom" or "religious liberty" have been a constant in our history, yet in differing historical contexts they have somewhat different referents, different overtones. Though there is certain consistency in their basic meaning across the centuries of Baptist history, they have carried somewhat different freight in changing historical moments. The princi-

---

[1]This article represents the Carver-Barnes Lecture, Southeastern Baptist Theological Seminary, given on 6 November 1984.

ple has also been very important in some other religious traditions which have
had their own distinctive histories so that various meanings get attached to it.
Also, the differing historical experiences of various nations have given particular twists to the way the concept of religious freedom is understood. For
example, as my beloved former colleague M. Searle Bates put it in his book
on religious liberty, ''Americans carelessly identify religious liberty with the
separation of Church from State, believing that the latter is the sole and necessary ground of the former.''[2] Yet a moment's reflection will call to mind
places in the world where religious freedom is effectively denied yet where
there is separation of church and state—a hostile separation. A twentieth-century writer laments that '' . . . the quasi-universal acceptance of the principle
of religious liberty is distorted in practice by the tremendous confusions concerning what liberty is, and what it ought to be.''[3] But to try to discuss the
matter on too broad a scale is to run the risk of drifting into vague generali-
ties, and so, endeavoring to be consistent with my point that the historical
situation in which one finds oneself does exert some influence on what one
does, I want to focus primarily on the Baptist principle of religious freedom
as it has been illumined and enlarged by changing historical contexts through
several centuries.

Those early English Baptists that gathered themselves together into a
congregation while in exile in Amsterdam were faced with a legally established church in the mother country which denied their right to exist. For them
the cry for religious liberty was for some space in which they could be free
to follow the teachings of the Bible and the guidance of the Spirit as they felt
led; it was also a protest against the oppressive power of the realities of historic European Christendom with its monolithic state-church systems. Because they were a tiny group of dissenters against a mighty power, their
statements often set their positive affirmations in a context of resistance. So
in an early declaration they exclaimed, ''The magistrate is not to meddle with
religion or matters of conscience, nor compel men to this or that form of religion; because Christ is the King and Law-giver of the Church and conscience.'' Despite the dangers, a number of the Baptists returned to their
homeland, to the England of James I, to whom in 1614 one of them, Leonard
Busher, addressed a petition entitled *Religions Peace: Or a Plea for Liberty
of Conscience*. Courageously he sketched out the view of a then tiny minority:

Kings and magistrates are to rule temporal affairs by the swords of their

---

[2]M. Searle Bates, *Religious Liberty: An Inquiry* (New York, 1945) 89.

[3]A. F. Carillo de Albornoz, in World Council of Churches, Division of Studies *Bulletin*,
9 (Spring, 1963): 19.

temporal kingdoms, and bishops and ministers are to rule spiritual affairs
by the Word and Spirit of God, the sword of Christ's spiritual kingdom, and
not to intermeddle one with another's authority, office, and function. . . .
It is not only unmerciful, but unnatural and abominable, yes, monstrous, for
one Christian to vex and destroy another for difference and questions of religion.[4]

Though we do not know much about Busher, the evidence indicates that he
was later cast into prison where he died several years after writing his bold
petition. In this and many other calls for religious freedom the then radical
suggestion that the spheres of civil and religious authority be separated was
often met by imprisonment. Relief came in the Cromwellian period, but in
the Restoration of 1660 Baptists and other nonconformists again felt the lash
of persecution for another three decades, and though the Toleration Act of
1689 ended the worst of it, the dissenters in England suffered under various
disabilities until the late 19th century.

Though religious traditions do change over time, the experiences of formative years usually set a mark on them not easily effaced, for memories are
somehow carried in a movement's life-stream so that persons who become
part of it later often share in the remembrance of events long past through
hidden channels that are difficult to trace. The early longing for freedom to
follow what they were convinced was the will of God but which so often
brought imprisonment and banishment gave Baptist people a keen distrust of
the mingling of religious and political power and of legal establishments of
religion, and in their historical experience pointed to separation of church and
state as an important means for securing religious freedom.

When the movement was still very young some who were Baptists or were
soon to become such joined in the great wave of migration to North America,
but they still found themselves within the bounds of Christendom with its patterns of legally established religion. As that colorful, provocative figure in
the renascence of Puritan studies, the late Perry Miller, once put it, "No nation of Europe had yet divided the state from the church; no government had
yet imagined that religion could be left to the individual conscience. Society,
economics, and the will of God were one and the same, and the ultimate authority in human relations was the ethic of Christendom."[5] Sometimes it
comes as a surprise to people to find that in no less than nine of the original
thirteen colonies that became the United States there were legal establishments of religion. They varied in type and effectiveness, but they were able

---

[4]Both quotations from Anson Phelps Stokes, *Church and State in the United States*, 3
vols. (New York, 1950) 1:113.

[5]Perry Miller, *Errand into the Wilderness* (New York, 1956) 105.

to tax, whip, harass, imprison, banish, and in a few cases to execute dissenters. Indeed, when the period of legal establishment finally ended—not until the early nineteenth century in three New England states—the general reaction against it was so strong few could remember why its patterns had been so powerful and had such a hold over people. In his last book, the historian Richard Hofstadter long puzzled over that mystery, digging into books and pamphlets now forgotten except by the specialists, and finally wrote a lucid paragraph that gives us a glimpse of the appeal of establishment Christendom. He wrote,

> An establishment in a healthy condition is intimately linked, . . . to the power of the state. Its ranks supply a parallel hierarchy of authority, which both supports and is supported by the secular power. . . . It commands the ready and willing allegiance of the majority of the population, for whom it is the inherited, the normal church; the agencies of education, charity, and welfare are in its hands; its local churches stand at the center of community life, and in the rhythms of daily existence it supplies the beat and tolls the bells. It is the core of the whole national system of values, spiritual, intellectual, and political, and it provides them with their distinctive texture.[6]

It took courage and determination to see the flaws in such a system and to stand against them, but representatives of the left wing of the Reformation, primarily the Mennonites, and of the left wing of Puritanism, especially Separatists, Baptists and Quakers, did that so as to be free to follow what they were convinced was the divine will in matters of faith.

There was a price to pay for standing against such a system, and throughout the colonial period many of them paid it. While still a Separatist, Roger Williams paid it as he was banished from Massachusetts Bay and fled in the depth of winter to found what has been called the first secular state in western history because it did separate state and church, and in his rather crabbed style he wrote books providing scriptural and theological arguments for religious freedom. Though he was one of the founders of the first Baptist church in America, his continuing religious pilgrimage led him into seekerism, but his originality in arguing for freedom and his actions in putting his ideas to work have understandably made him one of our heroes. Many others paid the price for standing against religious establishment—who can forget those four Quakers, one a woman, who perished on the gallows on Boston Common? And the price was still being paid by Baptists through the eighteenth century as they stood against both Congregational and Episcopal establishments. Even after our predecessors had begun to grow into one of the larger denominations, especially as they took the message and style of the Great Awakening

---

[6]Richard Hofstadter, *America at 1950: A Social Portrait* (New York, 1971) 204-205.

to heart, they were despised and persecuted as a fringe sect. In a historic treatment of the Great Awakening in Virginia, one scholar found that they were regarded as lawbreakers and a menace to society because their doctrines were subversive of religion and morality; they were called homebreakers, and their leaders were labelled false prophets whose piety was a sham.[7] How prejudiced people were against Baptists is revealed in a story from colonial Virginia repeated a few years ago by Walter Bronlow Posey. The story, which Posey called "delightful," is about an old Anglican woman who, when she encountered Baptists for the first time, exclaimed that "hardly any of them looked like other people." Her descriptive phrases for them were hardly flattering: "hair-lipped," "clump-footed," "blear eyed," "bow legged," and "hump-backed."[8] But however they were perceived by others, they were ready when their opportunity came during the Revolutionary War and in the period of drawing up constitutions that followed, and they made the most of it.

By then they were numerous enough to have some clout as they pressed for religious freedom; as Winthrop S. Hudson notes, "Between 1770 and 1800 Baptists emerged from relative obscurity to become the largest denomination in America."[9] They also had found some very effective leaders for their cause, notably Isaac Backus. Reared in the patterns of established Congregationalism in Massachusetts but converted to evangelical views early in the Great Awakening, Backus withdrew from his ancestral religious moorings to form a New Light church, and then moved on once again to form a Baptist church in 1756 and was ordained pastor over it, serving it for fifty years. William G. McLoughlin has edited a very useful collection of his pamphlets, identifying one he wrote in 1773, *An Appeal to the Public for Religious Liberty Against the Oppressions of the Present Day*, as "the most complete and well-rounded exposition of the Baptist principles of church and state in the eighteenth century. It owes something to Locke, a little to Roger Williams, a great deal to the Bible, and much to the historical experience of the Separate-Baptists since 1750."[10] As Baptists up and down the colonies participated in the struggle for independence, incidentally considerably improving what we would now call their public image, they sought every opportunity to press for religious

---

[7]Wesley M. Gewehr, *The Great Awakening in Virginia, 1740-1790* (Durham, 1930) 128-33.

[8]William Bronlow Posey, *Religious Strife on the Southern Frontier* (Baton Rouge, 1965) xvi-xvii.

[9]Winthrop S. Hudson, "Baptists, the Pilgrim Fathers, and the American Revolution," in James E. Wood, Jr. ed., *Baptists and the American Experience* (Valley Forge, 1976) 25.

[10]William G. McLoughlin, ed., *Isaac Backus on Church, State, and Calvinism: Pamphlets, 1754-1789* (Cambridge, MA, 1968) 41-42.

freedom. They teamed up with those of quite different religious views, often those inclined to rationalism, in the effort to move closer to the ideal of religious liberty in state after state. Though in such general treatments as this one, attention quickly gets focused on the dramatic changes affecting the religious situation at the national level, it is worth remembering that many of the important fights were in the villages and towns. In McLoughlin's words, "it was at the local level that compromises with dissenters were first worked out and the earliest and most important concessions won. The fight for religious liberty was primarily a neighborhood affair—a series of dialogues and face to face confrontations in church, parish, and town meetings which continued over two hundred years."[11] But the struggle at the top was important too; Baptists saw that Backus got to the federal Constitutional Convention in Philadelphia in 1787, and he was then influential in urging some of his dubious brethren to vote for ratification, especially because of its Article VI, that "no religious test shall ever be required as a qualification to any office or public trust under the United States."

There were many persons in America who thought that a further safeguard was needed, and so in their first session in 1789 the Senate and the House of Representatives worked out those sixteen fateful words that form the two clauses on religion that appear at the beginning of the First Amendment to the Constitution, "Congress shall make no law respecting an establishment of religion, or prohibiting the free exercise thereof." We do not have a complete record of those debates, but there are summaries and synopses of various speeches, discussions, and actions in the annals of Congress.[12] In the long wrangles over the issues in Congress in August and September of 1789, and then in the two years of discussion across the young nation until Virginia ratified the first ten amendments on December 17, 1791, thereby putting them into effect, I find that three main perspectives can be discerned, three main positions within which there were some variations but which can be quite clearly delineated.[13]

The first perspective was strongly shaped by the thought of the Enlightenment, so influential in the eighteenth century. Notable representatives of this position were such prominent leaders as Thomas Jefferson and James Madison. Jefferson, who at various times called himself a Deist, a Theist, a

---

[11]William G. McLoughlin, *New England Dissent, 1630-1833: The Baptists and the Separation of Church and State*, 2 vols. (Cambridge, MA, 1971) 1:xvii.

[12]*Journal of the First Session of the Senate of the United States of America . . . 1789* (New York, 1789) 116-51; cf. a summary interpretation by R. Freeman Butts, *The American Tradition in Religion and Education* (Boston, 1950) 72-79.

[13]I have developed these points more fully in an article, "The Magna Charta of Religious Freedom in America," *Union Seminary Quarterly Review*, 38 (1984): 301-17.

Unitarian and a rational Christian, displayed the Enlightenment's characteristic emphasis on natural rather than revealed religion in his famous "Bill for Establishing Religious Freedom," framed in 1777 and finally enacted with minor changes in his native state nine years later. Madison is not so easy to classify religiously because he was reluctant to speak about such matters; he was a regular attendant at Episcopal services, but as a student of Presbyterian John Witherspoon at Princeton he had been schooled in the teachings of the Scottish Enlightenment. His intense devotion to religious freedom was displayed especially in his powerful "Memorial and Remonstrance Against Religious Assessments," in which he insisted that freedom for one meant freedom for all when he said that "Whilst we assert for ourselves a freedom to embrace, to profess and to observe the Religion which we believe to be of divine origin, we cannot deny an equal freedom to those whose minds have not yet yielded to the evidence which has convinced us."[14] It was Madison who prepared the first draft of what became the Bill of Rights, who participated vigorously in the Congressional discussions in 1789, and who almost certainly wrote the final form of the First Amendment. Others, less conspicuous than these two but also often among the elites of that time, were also deeply informed by the Enlightenment perspective.

The second group was a much larger one and was of growing strength in the various strata of American society; elsewhere I have called them the dissenters, meaning that they disagreed with the views that had been held by the majority of Americans in the colonial period that religion should be legally established in some form or other. Most Baptists, of course, clearly worked from this perspective, along with Mennonites, Separate Congregationalists, Quakers and some other smaller groups which had played important roles in the four colonies which did not have religious establishments: Rhode Island, New Jersey, Pennsylvania, and Delaware. All these were among the people who often carried on the struggles for religious freedom at local levels, in the small villages and expanding towns.

The third perspective was important at the time, though it is easy to miss as we look back for we tend to focus on the outspoken figures who spoke for the first two positions. This third view was a more middle of the road one; let's call it the accommodationist perspective. Because of the growing religious pluriformity of the time, some persons who were not greatly troubled by establishments of religion nevertheless saw that a federal establishment of religion was not really possible or wise. Though they wanted to retain their state establishments, they accommodated to the general trend toward free-

---

[14]As reprinted by Saul K. Padover, ed., *The Complete Madison: His Basic Writings* (New York, 1953) 300-302.

dom by letting other denominations share in them through some form of "multiple establishment." Others that can be put in the same general category came from European traditions that had long been establishmentarian, but their historical experiences led them to opt in America for religious freedom. Its values for the North American setting had come to be recognized by such large bodies as the Presbyterian and small ones as the Roman Catholic. For example, the first American Catholic bishop, John Carroll, spoke many times of his "earnest regard to preserve inviolate forever in our new empire the great principle of religious liberty."[15] In Maryland, state leaders were willing to give up the Church of England establishment for denominational equality before the law in 1776, thus letting go of the design for a confessional state, for they saw that a generally Christian state was possible under the conditions of freedom.[16] Hence many persons from the accommodationist perspective had no trouble going along with the First Amendment but thought it would be favorable for their interests. As Mark DeWolfe Howe has summarized the matter, "among the most important purposes of the First Amendment was the advancement of the interests of religion."[17] Many sensed that it would open a new door of opportunity. Though this three-fold summary is something of an oversimplification, it does underline the fact that those who prepared the religion clauses of the First Amendment and then those who voted for and ratified them had different reasons for their actions.

In the context of that time, establishment was generally understood to mean the legal establishment of a church or churches, and Congress was forbidden to take any such step—or from prohibiting any one or any group from the free exercise of their religion. No wonder Baptists, who not many years before had known the realities of persecution, soon came to be ardent supporters of the amendment. The words "separation of church and state" were not in the amendment but soon were used to interpret it, especially after Jefferson's famous "wall of separation" letter to the Danbury Baptists in 1802.[18] The national trend toward religious freedom was soon felt in the states where establishment continued for a time; the last one succumbed only in 1833, though it was not for more than a century later in the 1940 *Cantwell* v. *Connecticut* case that the Supreme Court explicitly applied the free exercise clause

---

[15]As quoted by Peter Guilday, *The Life and Times of John Carroll*, 2 vols. (New York, 1922) 1:368.

[16]Thomas O'Brien Hanley, *The American Revolution and Religion: Maryland, 1770-1800* (Washington, 1971) 43-60.

[17]Mark DeWolfe Howe, *The Garden and the Wilderness: Religion and Government in American Constitutional History* (Chicago, 1965) 31.

[18]As cited by John F. Wilson, ed., *Church and State in American History* (Boston, 1965) 75-76.

to the states through the due process clause of the Fourteenth Amendment, and seven years later in *Everson* v. *Board of Education* did the same for the "no establishment" clause.

Meanwhile the churches flourished in a remarkable way through the nineteenth and into the twentieth centuries; the voluntary approach worked well for them. Despite smoldering and bitter anti-Catholicism that occasionally erupted into violence, the Roman Catholic Church grew rapidly, primarily through immigration, to become the single largest denomination by mid-nineteenth century. And Baptists, now out of the wilderness of legal establishment that had so long plagued them, especially flourished, becoming eventually the largest of the Protestant denominational families in the land. They became zealous defenders of the religion clauses of the First Amendment, finding them to be a proper way to protect that principle of religious freedom that was so precious to them.

Some, however, too easily overlooked the biblical and theological bases of the principle of religious freedom that had long marked the Baptist perspective to draw on the rationalistic and individualistic emphases, in part an extension of Enlightenment motifs that became so important in nineteenth century popular thought. There was a tendency to emphasize the negative aspects of freedom to stress freedom as absence of any external control over the individual, thus minimizing the theological context out of which the principle of religious freedom among Baptists had been developed and sustained. As the late C. Emanuel Carlson, a professor of history who later served more than fifteen years as the executive director of the Baptist Joint Committee on Public Affairs, once put it to a Baptist audience:

> It is precisely Jefferson's wall, and the undue attention we have paid to it, which has brought us to the place where all content has often been drained out of religious freedom as a positive force. We have been so preoccupied with our watch upon the wall, so paranoid about some supposed establishment of religion which somebody or other was trying to erect, that we have forgotten that the purpose of religion and the purpose of Christ for his church is that we should be free. But free for what? Free do to what?[19]

While such a critical reflection and questioning as that is before us, we might mention also several other limitations of views of religious freedom that flaw some pages of our history, such as the reluctance to extend it to native or black Americans in all too many cases. Some of the difficult chapters of history do make hard reading—but they can help us to examine our own views and practices in the realization that as we are critical of some of the limitations of our

---

[19]C. Emanuel Carlson, "The Meaning of Religious Liberty," in Wood, ed., *Baptists and the American Experience* 210.

forebears so later our views and deeds may be scrutinized by those who come after us.

In a few years we will be observing the 200th anniversary of the First Amendment, long such an important statement for Baptists. How different is the nation today from what it was nearly two centuries ago—it has increased some four times in geographical area and nearly sixty times in population, and the spectrum of religious bodies, then predominantly Protestant, has widened astonishingly in number and variety to include quite complex denominational families not even then in existence. The character of our separation of church and state has changed; it was through most of the nineteenth century and into the twentieth predominantly a benevolent separation; it has become increasingly neutralist in the later twentieth century and some fear it may turn hostile. Persons of various religious perspectives point out that certain actions by local, state, and national bureaucracies may be based on increasingly narrow definitions of what religion is, thereby in fact infringing on the free exercise clause.[20] Confusions exist as to what separation of church and state is; several years ago when the Roman Catholic Archbishop of Chicago died, I was startled to read a newspaper article of which the lead sentence read "John Cardinal Cody, who died April 25, never really bought the idea of the separation of church and state."[21] The rest of the article spoke only of the late cardinal's forthright stands on moral and ethical issues, including his actions on behalf of racial integration. There was not another word after that first sentence about church-state issues; it was simply assumed, wrongly, that strong words and action on public issues by a church leader violated the separation of church and state. Though I suspect historical precedent will prevent anything being done about it, the very phrase "separation of church and state" may no longer point to the current realities as much as some such clumsy phrase like the "separation of religious bodies and governmental agencies" might. McLoughlin found that the fight for religious liberty in seventeenth and eighteenth centuries was primarily a neighborhood affair; the struggle in the late twentieth to maintain it may once again be carried on at a local level.

From the point of view of Baptist history and thought, the basic principle at stake is religious freedom, and what we have called the separation of church and state is a way to protect and extend the principle. When the one hundredth anniversary of the adoption of the American Constitution was celebrated almost a hundred years ago, the leading church historian in America, Philip Schaff, called the First Amendment "the Magna Charta of religious freedom

---

[20]E.g., cf. Dean M. Kelley, ed., *Government Intervention in Religious Affairs* (New York, 1982).

[21]Joseph A. Reaves, "Cardinal Cody Spoke His Mind Faithfully," *Buffalo News*, 2 May 1982.

in the United States,'' for it meant that the new nation had furnished ''the first example in history of a government deliberately depriving itself of all legislative control over religion.''[22] To be sure religious freedom can mean freedom *from* religion, and those who insist on that are protected by it. More subtly, however, it can be used by quite sincere believers to try to hide from the searching divine spirit when in our pride we claim our freedom to follow our own narrow self-interests without submitting them to the judgment of our brothers and sisters in Christ or even seriously to our God in prayer. We may misuse our freedom as a screen behind which we pay attention primarily to our own private or institutional concerns and neglect some of the more important matters about which the gospel speaks. If we turn some of our attention to seeking justice for those who have been treated unjustly or in working for a more equitable distribution of the rich resources of earth, then we may quickly find that many inside the church and outside do not want us to use our freedom in that way, for they have consciously or unconsciously understood religious freedom as a way of keeping the gospel out of harm's way, sealed off from making annoying claims that might call for serious alignments in our various human systems. The First Amendment still protects us on the human level to stand fast in the freedom with which Christ has set us free; if it were taken away we'd have to go to work with others to provide something like it all over again.

The greatest danger to religious freedom today might just come from those who have it and do not use it. If we believe that God is at work to free humanity from the burdens of sinfulness and oppression, then we are called to invest our freedom, even to risk it by doing the work the Lord has called us to do. But however precious it is, religious freedom is neither the first nor the second commandment, it is not the call to love God and the neighbor. It is a principle, central in the Baptist tradition, a principle invoked so that persons and groups can respond to the divine call as it comes to them, and can reach out to others without hindrance in witness and service. We invoke that principle for ourselves and others because we love and trust the loving God made known in Christ.

---

[22]Philip Schaff, *Church and State in the United States* (New York, 1888) 22-23.

ISAAC BACKUS: EIGHTEENTH CENTURY LIGHT ON THE CONTEMPORARY SCHOOL PRAYER ISSUE

STANLEY J. GRENZ
NORTH AMERICAN BAPTIST SEMINARY
SIOUX FALLS SD 57105

Two decades after the landmark Supreme Court cases of 1962 and 1963, public school prayer has remained a controversial and significant church-state issue. During his first term, President Reagan raised this explosive question himself. In fact, he became the first president since the decisions of the early 1960's to recommend adoption of a constitutional amendment on prayer in the nation's classrooms. Congressional discussion of the Reagan-supported proposal climaxed in the 19 March 1984 Senate vote in which proponents failed to obtain the two-thirds majority needed for passage. Since that vote, the Senate has been called on to debate the merits of yet another constitutional amendment. The newer proposal (S.J. Res.2), which was approved by the Senate Judiciary Committee in October 1985, refers specifically to silent prayer: ''Nothing in this Constitution shall be construed to prohibit individual or group silent prayer or reflection in public schools . . . ''

Public school prayer has become an emotion-filled and devisive issue, not only in the political area, but also within the religious community. Even the Baptists, who have historically stood at the forefront of religious liberty causes in America, have not been able to find agreement on this question. On the one hand, agencies such as the Baptist Joint Committee on Public Affairs support the Supreme Court decisions of 1960s and oppose the various attempts to reintroduce some form of government-sponsored school prayer. On the other hand, several well-known Baptists are among the most outspoken supporters of the President's amendment as well as the entire New Right agenda. On the surface at least, this cleavage appears to be a baffling contradiction.

In this situation of internal cleavage, Baptist history can be of great assistance both in gaining an understanding of the current division on the prayer issue and in seeking a way through the current impasse. One period of Baptist history which is highly instructive is eighteenth century New England. Although the efforts of Roger Williams in the seventeenth century had secured a charter for Rhode Island which granted religious freedom to all, the struggle for religious liberty in New England and in the colonies as a whole intensified in the eighteenth century. This later struggle, more so than Williams' pioneer work, opened the way for the experiment in church-state separation that the American nation came to accept. The Baptist fight against religious taxation in eighteenth century New England, a fight which in part paved the way for separation of church and state, was spearheaded by a Massachusetts pastor named Isaac Backus.

Backus was born into a Connecticut Congregationalist family in 1726. As a teenager he and his family joined the ranks of the New Lights (those who were touched by the revivalism of the Great Awakening). Soon young Backus was called as pastor of a Separate congregation (i.e., an unauthorized church made up of New Lights who had left the government-supported parish church) in a new settlement near Middleboro, Massachusetts. Several years later Backus became convinced of the immersionist position, a conviction which eventually caused him to dissolve his congregation and form a Baptist church in Middleboro. First as a Separate and then as a Baptist he witnessed the suffering which religious dissenters in New England were forced to bear. By the time of the American Revolution, Backus had concluded that the plight of his co-religionists would be remedied only by total disestablishment of the dominant Congregational churches.

Backus' realization of the necessity of disestablishment presented him with the task of developing a theory of church-state relations that could undergird and explicate the separation of the two spheres which he advocated. In the construction of his theory he drew upon the philosophy of John Locke and the Calvinism mediated to him by the eminent theologian, Jonathan Edwards. Although acquainted with and appreciative of the viewpoints and writings of Baptists in both Old and New England including Roger Williams, Backus utilized these resources sparingly. His theory was more a personal synthesis of the Enlightenment and Puritanism with an eye to the heritage of

his adopted denomination than a mere restating of traditional Baptist out-
looks.

In the closing decades of the eighteenth century Backus' viewpoint on
church-state separation resonated well with the work of certain of his contem-
poraries. Finally the loose coalition of Baptists and Virginia laditudinarians
(e.g., Jefferson, Madison, etc.) prevailed, and the nation as a whole accepted
disestablishment. Since he was the leading theorist and spokesman of the New
England Baptists, Backus also became an important architect of the church-
state system which was employed by the new American nation.

Backus was first and foremost a Christian pastor. Therefore, it is not surprising that theological conviction lay at the heart of his church-state theory.
Specifically, three doctrines formed its foundation. First, his starting point
was found in the grand Calvinist emphasis on the sovereignty of God. For
Backus, God was the governor of the universe to whom all earthly civil governments must appeal for legitimization.[1] Human government was thereby
declared to be God's creation, instituted to fulfill a divinely-given task.

The second central doctrine in Backus' theory was anthropology. He followed Locke and Edwards in emphasizing the human intellect as the con-
trolling faculty of the individual.[2] Drawing on this emphasis and on Calvinist
influences, Backus defined human freedom as the ability to act consistent with
reason.[3]

Backus combined this basic anthropology with the Biblical stories of creation and fall to produce an elaborate understanding of the human predica-
ment, which was quite similar to that devised by Edwards. The human person
was created to be governed by ''reason and a well-informed judgment,''
Backus declared, which would be influenced by the command to love God.
But then another ''external motive,'' ''the conceit that man could advance
either his honor or happiness by disobedience instead of obedience,'' was injected by ''the father of lies.'' This evil imagination ''usurped'' the place of
a properly informed reason, a usurpation which continues in the history of
every human being. The result of this is depravity, as individual reason is no
longer given the position of leadership over personal actions. Liberty consists
in the ability to hinder one's own desires from determining one's will until
the good and evil of the proposed action has been examined.[4] For this, divine

---

[1]Isaac Backus, *Truth is Great and Will Prevail* (Boston, 1781), in William McLoughlin,
ed., *Isaac Backus on Church, State, and Calvinism: Pamphlets, 1754-1789* (Cambridge, Mass.:
Harvard University Press, 1968) 402.

[2]Backus, *The Sovereign Decree of God* (Boston, 1773), in *Pamphlets* 297.

[3]Backus, *The Doctrine of Sovereign Grace Opened and Vindicated* (Providence, R.I.,
1771) 60-62.

[4]Ibid., 61-62.

influence is needed, mediated to the individual by the Scriptures, which are designed to act against the "evil imaginations" and to combat ignorance, thereby bringing freedom.[5] This divine assistance results in faith, the acceptance of the truth about God and humanity, which occurs whenever the gospel proclamation (that is, the demands of God in the law plus the saving work of Christ) is so pressed by the Holy Spirit on an individual that the conscience is pricked, and the mind, impressed with the reasonableness of the message, embraces its truth.

In this, Backus' stress on the particular individual rather than the corporate being is evident. In his understanding, it is the individual in whom reason was originally designed to rule. Likewise, it is the individual whom the Holy Spirit teaches the truths of God's Word. For these reasons, the Middleboro minister concluded, "religion is ever a matter between God and individuals,"[6] "true religion is a voluntary obedience unto God,"[7] and each one is individually answerable to God, both as judge[8] and, for the Christian, as master ("to his own master each soul stands or falls"[9]). In short, religion is a relationship between the individual and God, mediated only by Holy Spirit illumined Scripture.

The third central doctrine in Backus' church-state theory was ecclesiology, that is, the doctrine of the church itself. Although agreeing with his opponents' dichotomy between the visible and invisible churches, Backus conceived of the visible church as a voluntary society of believers,[10] an idea for which he found precedence in Locke.[11] This voluntary society consisted in the local congregation formed by a voluntary covenant of its members,[12] and not in the parish churches which had developed in New England. In this way the stress on the individual found in Backus' anthropology was paralleled by a stress on the individual in the formation of the covenant church community.

---

[5]Backus, *The Doctrine of Particular Election and Final Perserverance* (Boston, 1789), in *Pamphlets* 451.

[6]Backus, *Door Opened for Religious Liberty* (Boston, 1778), in *Pamphlets* 432.

[7]Backus, *Government and Liberty Described* (Boston, 1778), in *Pamphlets* 351.

[8]Backus, *Truth is Great and Will Prevail* 414.

[9]Backus, *A Short Description of the Differences between the Bondwoman and the Free* (Boston, 1756), in *Pamphlets* 163.

[10]Backus, *Door Opened for Religious Liberty* 432.

[11]Backus, *Policy as Well as Honesty Forbids the Use of Secular Force in Religious Affairs* (Boston, 1779), in *Pamphlets*, p. 376. Here Backus quotes John Locke, *A Letter Concerning Toleration*, 3rd ed. (Boston, 1743) 17.

[12]Backus, *A History of New England*, second edition (Newton, Mass., 1871) 2:304.

Out of these three foundational doctrines grew Backus' theory of church and state. This theory contained three basic theses. First, for Backus governmental structure is intrinsic to human existence. This thesis developed out of Backus' understanding of God's design for humanity. The human person was created to exist under both the external providential governance of the Creator and the internal governance of personal reason. This being the case, concluded Backus, government and liberty cannot be incompatible.[13] Human government, then, is God's agent in the face of human rebellion (sin) against the divine governance.[14]

Backus' second thesis declared that God had instituted two different governments, the civil and the ecclesiastical, each one with differing tasks and spheres of responsibility. He wrote, ''Men have three things to be concerned for, namely, soul, body and estate. The two latter belong to the magistrate's jurisdiction, the other does not.''[15] In its divinely-given task the civil government has two basic duties, according to Backus. On the one hand it must ''punish such as work ill to their neighbor.'' To carry out this duty, and this one alone, the magistrate ''bears the sword.''[16] On the other hand ''all who are in authority'' are to ''protect and encourage such a quiet and peaceable life in all Godliness and honesty.''[17]

Although Backus acknowledged certain structural similarities between the two governments, he underscored one major difference between them. In contrast to the church, in the civil sphere ''dominion'' is not ''founded in grace.'' In this declaration Backus was rejecting a popular viewpoint of his day, that ''religion endows the subjects of it with a right to act as lawgivers and judges over others.''[18] In his understanding the civil government is to defend its citizens against the hostilities of others and to promote upright living by means of respectable magistrates elected by the entire population regardless of religious persuasion.

Distinct from civil government in Backus' theory is the ecclesiastical, with jurisdiction over human souls.[19] For him the distinction between the two governments is based on the inward nature of religion as opposed to the outward

---

[13]Backus, *An Appeal to the Public for Religious Liberty* (Boston, 1773), in *Pamphlets* 309,312.

[14]Backus, *A History of New England* 2:321.

[15]Backus, *Policy as Well as Honesty* 381.

[16]Backus, *A History of New England* 2:265.

[17]Backus, *An Address to the Inhabitants of New England* (Boston, 1787), in *Pamphlets* 446.

[18]Backus, *A History of New England* 2:373.

[19]Ibid., 2:561.

nature of civil jurisdiction. He saw precedence for this not only in Locke,[20] but more importantly in Christ himself, who according to Backus commanded the church, ''Put away from among yourselves that wicked person,'' but said to the state, ''Let both (i.e., the wheat and the tares) grow together until the harvest'' (here he cited 1 Cor 5:13; Matt 13:30, 38-43).[21]

The distinction between the civil and ecclesiastical governments suggested to Backus that there be a twofold separation of the two. On the one hand the church must not interfere in the civil sphere. This is demanded by the Lord's exclusion of the sword from his kingdom[22] and by the nature of religion itself. On the other hand, an even worse threat must be avoided, that of interference in the ecclesiastical by the civil, which takes the form of the use of secular force in religious affairs. According to Backus those who are guilty of this ''violate the divine command both ways; they obstruct discipline in the church, and invade the rights of conscience and humanity in the State.''[23]

Although Backus advocated some form of separation of church and state, the separation he envisioned did not require competition between the two spheres. In fact, since both are God's institutions, a harmonious relationship, a ''sweet harmony,'' ought to exist:

> . . . as civil rulers ought to be men fearing God, and hating covetousness, and to be terrors to evil doers, and a praise to them who do well; and as ministers ought to pray for rulers, and to teach the people to be subject to them, so there may and ought to be a sweet harmony between them. . . . [24]

In the same way, the separation he proposed did not deny the importance of religion to the well-being of society:

> the necessity of a well-regulated government in civil states is acknowledged by all, and the importance and benefit of true Christianity in order thereto is no less certain. For the great Author of it assures us that his disciples are the salt of the earth and the light of the world, Matt. vi, 13, 14. That is, his religion is as necessary for the well-being of human society as salt is to preserve from putrefaction or as light is to direct our way to guard against enemies, confusion and misery.[25]

What separation did mean was that no civil government has the right to seek

---

[20]Backus, *Seasonable Plea for Liberty of Conscience* (Boston, 1770) 12.

[21]Backus, *Policy as Well as Honesty* 375. *Doctrine of Particular Election* 468.

[22]Backus, *Policy as Well as Honesty* 382.

[23]Backus, *A History of New England* 2:74.

[24]Backus, *A Fish Caught in His Own Net* (Boston, 1768), in *Pamphlets* 190-91.

[25]Backus, *Policy as Well as Honesty* 371.

to secure legislatively the benefits of religion.[26] Backus went so far as to question whether those benefits can actually be attained by such means. All civil legislation entails coersion, but religion by its very nature must be uncoerced.

Backus advocated a different means of securing the piety necessary to society. Rather than legislating religion, the civil government must limit its role to that of creating a climate in which truth is free to act. Piety in turn is guaranteed to society by the sovereign God through the convincing power of truth by means of the missionary enterprise of the church. As individuals are converted they become good citizens. He wrote, "if the church of Christ were governed wholly by his laws, enforced in his name, she should be an infinite blessing to human society,"[27] for

> if all were protected impartially, they who act from heavenly motives would strengthen the hands of civil rulers, and hold up light to draw others out of evil ways, and to guard against all iniquity.[28]

Herein, then, is the "sweet harmony" between church and state: Christ is sovereign in his church and through his people draws the individual members of society to acknowledge the truth of Christianity, by which the state is benefited, because "real Christians are the best subjects of civil government in the world."[29]

The third thesis in Backus' church-state theory allowed for governmental activity in the moral realm, even though church matters lay beyond its role. Following Locke and the Enlightenment, he held to a "twofold source of truth," reason and revelation. Certain truths of morality and religion, this understanding declared, are present to all persons regardless of confessional persuasion, for these are mediated to all by human reason. This being the case, legislation in such areas is permitted. Such civil action does not entail a denial of religious liberty, since the citizen is merely forced thereby to act according to reason, which is freedom in the true sense. At the same time, however, other moral and religious truths are available only through special revelation. These lie outside the governance of the civil sphere.[30] In such matters the civil magistrate must give place to the convincing power of truth.

This, then, was the program outlined by Backus and adopted to a large extent by the new nation. Government is a legitimate institution derived from

---

[26]Ibid., 375.

[27]Backus, *The Kingdom of God Described by His Word* (Boston, 1792) 14.

[28]Backus, *A History of New England* 2:378.

[29]Backus, *An Abridgment of the Church History of New England* (Boston, 1804) 245.

[30]For a fuller discussion see Stanley J. Grenz, "Isaac Backus and Religious Liberty," *Foundations*, 22:4 (October-December 1979): 352-60.

God. The civil and religious spheres are distinct entities, separated in function and in fact. Morality, however, falls under the domain of both, being
divided into each sphere according to the twofold source of truth. Natural truth
of reason is to be legislated, whereas supernatural truth of revelation is to be
reserved for ecclesiastical jurisdiction.

Backus' theory of church-state separation forms an important background for an understanding of the cleavage among his denominational children over various contemporary church-state questions, including the school
prayer issue. The Middleboro minister divided morality into the jurisdiction
of church and state. This had the effect of dividing ethics into categories of
natural (reason) and supernatural (revelation). Unfortunately he did not de-
vise an eternally-valid means to delineate clearly where this division ought to
fall.

Backus left to his spiritual children a clear theory of church-state separation, yet one which is not unproblematic in specific application. This is seen
in various current Baptist debates, which tend to center less on church-state
theory (this is generally accepted by all) than on application of theory to specific issues. The discussion of public school prayer, for example, largely re-
volves around the question of the legitimacy of any governmental role in
supporting prayer. In terms of Backus' model the question becomes whether
or not prayer is a natural duty, a general good, and therefore within the
boundary of the civil government to advance.

That there are no easy answers to this question was evident already in
Backus' day. This issue constituted a point of controversy between himself
and the seventeenth century pioneer of religious liberty, Roger Williams.
Backus quoted approvingly a now famous paragraph from Williams' *History
of Providence*:

> I affirm that all the liberty of conscience, that ever I pleaded for, turns upon
> these two hinges, that none of the Papists, Protestants, Jews or Turks, be
> forced to come to the ship's prayers or worship; nor secondly compelled from
> their own particular prayers or worship, if they practice any. I further add,
> that I never denied that notwithstanding this liberty, the commander of this
> ship ought to command the ship's course; yea, and also command that jus-
> tice, peace and sobriety to be kept and practiced, both among the seamen
> and all the passengers. If any of the seamen refuse to perform their service,
> or passengers to pay their freight; if any refuse to help in person or purse
> towards the common charges or defense; if any refuse to obey the common
> laws and orders of the ship, concerning their common peace or preservation;
> if any shall mutiny and rise up against their commanders and officers; if any
> should (shall) preach or write that there ought to be no commanders nor of-
> ficers, because all are equal in Christ, therefore no masters nor officers, no
> laws nor orders, no corrections nor punishments; I say, I never denied but
> in such cases, whatever is pretended, the commander or commanders may

judge, resist, compel and punish such transgressors, according to their des-
erts and merits.[31]

This, commented Backus, is a "clear description of the difference between
civil and ecclesiastical affairs, and of the difference betwixt good government on the one hand, and tyranny or licentiousness on the other."[32] However, Backus parted company with his predecessor at one significant point:

> The light of nature teaches the importance of seeking to God for what we
> need, and of praising him for what we receive, which duties ought to be in-
> culcated upon all men, as much as love to God or our neighbors; while the
> revealed institutions of baptism and the supper, are tokens of fellowship with
> Christ, and therefore cannot be our duty to perform before we are united to
> him . . . But for awhile, Mr. Williams seemed to limit those two kinds of
> duties (i.e., petition and thanksgiving) alike to the regenerate.[33]

In Backus' understanding both he and Williams were in agreement that
the civil government has the right to demand that its citizens perform whatever moral duties are taught by natural religion. They differed, however, in
the relationship of prayer to human reason. Williams denied that prayer falls
under this category. But for Backus,

> Daily prayer to God for what we need, and praises for what we receive, are
> duties taught by reason as well as revelation; and every person is inexcus-
> able that neglects the immediate practice of these duties.[34]

Proponents of school prayer today could well interpret Backus' remarks
as favoring their position. According to the New Right, prayer is in some sense
subject to government sponsorship. This could be defended by Backus' suggestion that prayer is a common human duty taught by reason itself. Baptist
supporters of the Reagan amendment, therefore, rather than being totally at
variance with their heritage as some claim, do indeed to some degree stand
on the legacy of Isaac Backus, who was himself one of the architects of
American church-state theory.

At the same time, however, two additional observations must be considered before simply granting the case to the advocates of public school prayer.
First, the unfolding of subsequent history has revealed that Backus had pur-
chased too much from the Enlightenment. In the two hundred years since his
day it has been discovered that the "truths of reason" which he relegated to
the legislative power of civil government were little more than the moral con-

---

[31]Backus, *A History of New England* 1:238.

[32]Ibid.

[33]Ibid., 361.

[34]Ibid., 2:2.

sensus of the eighteenth century. Backus was living in a society in which religious doctrines such as the reality of God were widely accepted, and religious duties such as prayer were widely practiced. This caused many, including Backus, to conclude that they were universally taught by human reason.

The contemporary situation is far different. Lying between Backus and late twentieth century American society are two hundred years, which have witnessed the erosion of the religious consensus of his day. For this reason, any attempt to conclude with Backus that prayer is a natural truth taught by human reason and therefore under the jurisdiction of the state is highly questionable. History has shown Williams, not Backus, to have been the more perceptive of the two concerning the relationship between prayer and natural reason.

Secondly, however, Backus is not without insight for the current situation. The main thrust of his church-state theory continues to be helpful even in the present debate. Ultimately, religion is a matter of inward commitment, as Backus concluded from his anthropology and ecclesiology. Therefore, church and state do have fundamentally different tasks in society. Likewise, the inward basis of religious commitment undermines any legislative attempt to secure the benefits of piety for society as a whole.

Backus was surely correct in seeking to limit the role of civil government in religious issues to one of benign neutrality. Its task can only be that of providing a climate in which truth is free to accomplish its mission of convicting human minds. Government itself cannot advance the gospel. Therefore, it ought not to legislate purely religious practices. Backus rightly called on the civil sphere to allow the church, which has been charged by Christ with the mandates of evangelism and nurture, to do its work of teaching religious truth unhindered.

In the aftermath of the Supreme Court decisions of the 1960s, there have been many occasions in which the Court rulings have been utilized to suggest that all voluntary religious expressions in public schools are illegal.[35] In this way the civil government has been invoked in opposition to religion. Such action is contrary to Backus' understanding of the separation of church and state. According to Backus, civil government has the responsibility to create a climate in which truth is free to carry on its convincing task unhindered. Contemporary Baptists, therefore, do right in calling for the free exchange of ideas in the public schools. But since prayer is a purely religious exercise and not a truth taught by natural reason, as history has shown, the way to achieve the goal of creating a climate of freedom is not through the reintroduction of

---

[35]Such occasions are repeatedly cited in New Right literature. For example, a compilation of recent situations is found in Martin Mawyer, ''Religious Freedom not Welcomed in Public Places,'' *Fundamentalist Journal* 3:8 (September 1984): 61-62.

government-sponsored prayer, even of the ''voluntary'' type advocated by some Baptists today. True religion simply cannot be legislated.

One cannot dogmatically assert exactly how Isaac Backus would view the contemporary prayer question, if he were here today. In a very real sense he laid the theoretical groundwork for the New Right position which advocated prayer in public schools. At the same time his writings indicate that as perceptive a mind as his would have learned the lesson of the intervening years. Subsequent history might well have taught Backus that prayer is a purely religious expression and not a civil duty, a conclusion to which Williams had come a century earlier. This realization would have brought him to see that all government-sanctioned prayer constitutes an overstepping of the ''sweet harmony'' between the civil and ecclesiastical spheres, which Backus so forcefully advocated.

FUNDAMENTALISM AND THE SOUTH

SAMUEL S. HILL
UNIVERSITY OF FLORIDA
GAINESVILLE FL 32611

In this article the progression is from a description of religion to an examination of culture. In the first section the discussion centers on Evangelicalism and Fundamentalism as religious belief-systems and movements. The second section treats the setting provided by southern history and culture for the religious movements.

I. HOW FUNDAMENTALIST IS SOUTHERN RELIGION?

Is southern religion Fundamentalist? ''You've got to be kidding'' is the response of many to that apparently rhetorical question. Most Americans living outside the region think of it that way, and most media people are apt to generalize that the popular religion of the south is Fundamentalist.

By any precise characterizing, however, that is not the case. If the choice is limited to two, between Fundamentalism and Modernism (or liberalism), then of course the South is Fundamentalist. But in the main it really is not. What it is is Evangelical, in a variety of ways. The Evangelical family in Protestant Christianity is far larger than the body of conservative Christians called Fundamentalist. Indeed, of the 40 million Evangelicals, some four to five million are entitled to classification as Fundamentalists. We will be looking at definitions and descriptions of these two movements, but at the moment it is enough to say that Fundamentalists are radicals or extremists within the Evangelical community of Protestant Christianity.

Furthermore, Fundamentalism is a relatively recent phenomenon. As far as the South is concerned it did not emerge until several decades after southern religious patterns were set in place and a regional consensus had appeared about 1830, and then not initially in the South. With roots in the 1880s and 1890s, it took firm shape in the 1920s and 1930s. Its primary areas of development were in New England, New York state, and the upper Middle West. With reference to religious groups, it broke out inside the northern Presbyterian and Baptist denominations, and within newly created sectarian bodies of Holiness, millennialist, and Adventist people. For the first two-thirds of the nineteenth century, an Evangelical consensus held most (white) American Protestants within earshot of each other. However, from the time of Dwight L. Moody forward, the 1870s and 1880s, diverging streams were subdividing the Protestant community. Much of the conservative stream was withdrawn from and hostile to culture between the two great wars, thus fundamentalistic. That movement was relatively minor before 1915 and after 1942. The larger Evangelical community was continually shifting both in its internal alignments and in its attitudes toward the surrounding society and culture.

George Marsden offers these descriptions of what Fundamentalism was during this era of its first prominence in American society which comprised the larger share of Evangelical strength.

> From its origins fundamentalism was primarily a religious movement. It was a movement among American ''evangelical'' Christians, people professing complete confidence in the Bible and preoccupied with the message of God's salvation of sinners through the death of Jesus Christ. Evangelicals were convinced that sincere acceptance of this ''Gospel'' message was the key to virtue in this life and to eternal life in heaven; its rejection means following the broad path that ended with the tortures of hell. Unless we appreciate the immense implications of a deep religious commitment to such beliefs—implications for one's own life and for attitudes toward others—we cannot appreciate the dynamics of fundamentalist thought and action.

More specifically Marsden goes on to characterize Fundamentalism as an informal alliance set off by its sharp opposition to other brands of Christianity.

> During this period of its national prominence in the 1920s, fundamentalism is best defined in terms of these concerns. Briefly, it was militantly anti-modernist Protestant evangelicalism. Fundamentalists were evangelical Christians, close to the traditions of the dominant American revivalist establishment of the nineteenth century, who in the twentieth century militantly opposed both modernism in theology and the cultural changes that modernism endorsed. Militant opposition to modernism was what most clearly set off fundamentalism from a number of closely related traditions,

such as evangelicalism, revivalism, pietism, the holiness movements, millenarianism, Reformed confessionalism, Baptist traditionalism, and other denominational orthodoxies. Fundamentalism was a "movement" in the sense of a tendency or development in Christian thought that gradually took on its own identity as a patchwork coalition of representatives of other movements. Although it developed a distinct life, identity, and eventually a subculture of its own, it never existed wholly independently of the older movements from which it grew. Fundamentalism was a loose, diverse, and changing federation of co-belligerents united by their fierce opposition to modernist attempts to bring Christianity into line with modern thought.[1]

A tighter definition of Fundamentalism from a truly radical position within it is offered by George W. Dollar: "Historic fundamentalism is a literal exposition of all the affirmations and attitudes of the Bible and the militant exposure of all non-Biblical affirmations and attitudes." We should note then that hard-line Fundamentalism declares both a positive program and a negative program. It has its own agenda and it makes most others' agendas its own business.[2]

Getting our bearings, then, Fundamentalism is one kind of Evangelical Christianity. This means that: (1) all Fundamentalists are Evangelicals; (2) most Evangelicals are not Fundamentalists; (3) there are other versions of Evangelical Christianity than Fundamentalism.

The South's religious patterns, characteristically distinctive, prove to be so as well on the question of Evangelicalism and its Fundamentalist branch. ("distinctive" but not unique.) Four main versions or parties of Evangelicalism are present in the region. They are, ranging from most to least separatist and exclusivist, the Truth party, the Conversion party, the Spirituality party, and the Service party. Incidentally, Corwin Smidt, a Political Scientist at Wheaton, draws the distinction between Conversionist and Confessional Evangelicals.

(1) The Truth party magnifies correct belief. These kinds of conservative Christians stay to themselves, are not inclined to be cooperative, are apt to be anti-culture, and live and die by precision in definition and behavior. Prominent examples are independent Baptists and Churches of Christ, as different as those two groupings are (even within themselves). (2) The Conversion party gives priority to evangelism, the winning of "the lost" to faith in Christ. Thus they are aggressive in reaching out to the unconverted at home and the heathen in other cultures. The Southern Baptists make this the nu-

---

[1]George M. Marsden, *Fundamentalism and American Culture* (New York: Oxford University Press, 1980) 3,4.

[2]George W. Dollar, *A History of Fundamentalism in America* (Greenville, SC: Bob Jones University Press, 1973) v.

merically most popular form of Evangelicalism in the region, but other smaller groups too are powered by a passion for conversion.

(3) The Spirituality party stresses the constant and intimate presence of the Lord in the world and in one's personal life, Spiritual power is readily accessible for daily decisions, and awareness of God and, among some, for healing of body or speaking in tongues. Examples are certain kinds of Methodists, Pentecostals, and charismatics. The faith of black Christians, while distinctive, fits reasonably well in this category owing to its sense of God's nearness, the power of deliverance, and the impact of his joy on the soul. (4) The Service party has a small number of adherents but it is unmistakably southern. For Christians such as Will Campbell and the late Clarence Jordan (of Koinonia Farms), Evangelical faith determines life-style. It always calls for the embodiment of reconciliation, between races, classes, and peoples. It may also call for pacifism and economic communalism.

At least one other version is present on the national scene, "progressive" or "comprehensive" Evangelicalism. In general we may describe it as building a strong "service" motif on a very firm "truth" basis (often propositional revelation) with a vigorous sense of discipline in its spirituality, but without revivalism as the shape of its ministry of "conversion."

This "progressive" party is a small minority in the South. Moreover, southern and northern versions of the four parties described differ somewhat. But throughout this treatment, it is essential to note that these are not mutually exclusive manifestations of Evangelical faith; a great deal of overlapping or eclecticism may be present.

Fundamentalism belongs to the Truth party. Beyond what has been said already, we must note that it is rationalist. This is an instance of "head" religion. It may be anti-intellectual rationalism, but it is still rationalism. It believes that revelation is propositional, that God inspired accurate statements to the biblical authors. Correct belief is possible and and necessary because of the particular nature of the authoritative Scripture. Testing the orthodoxy of others is both possible and necessary.

Generally speaking, Fundamentalists hold to exactly the same doctrines as other Evangelicals—and even some Christians in the mainline churches. But they do so with a different attitude. That is, specific doctrines must be interpreted in specified ways. And they establish a check list in order to test and prove orthodoxy and authenticity. It is part of the mission of Fundamentalists to make other Christians' and other Christian denominations' point of view a matter for their scrutiny. A part of their calling is to expose error, heresy, heterodoxy, wherever it may appear among people who claim to be Christian (but of course deceive themselves and others).

Thus, they are divisive. They set out, of course, to be straight and true, not to produce division. But the Fundamentalists' *modus vivendi* leads to fragmenting, fracturing, or sundering, almost inevitably. Theirs is a differentiationist mentality; people who call themselves Christians are divided into two camps, the truth-sayers and the liars. As always with human groups, some Fundamentalists are more gracious, some are more strident than others. The manner of the assault on heretics varies in pace and intensity. Most Evangelicals incline toward classifying the human race as the "we" or "in" group over against the "them" or "out" group. The criteria can range from belief in sound doctrine to a conversion experience to the gifts of speaking in tongues. What Evangelicals generally merely "incline" toward typifies or defines Fundamentalist behavior. But there is diversity even here.

In the case of the Bob Jones and Carl McIntyre brands, the posture is absolutistic and judgmental and highly sectarian. Even other self-styled Fundamentalists are considered apostate, and the rest (the majority) of the Evangelicals are accused of compromise into liberalism. For Jerry Falwell and his group, the Baptist Bible Fellowship (with a college and offices in Springfield, Missouri), the assessment of others is somewhat less judgmental and a bit more gracious. With a third variety in the Truth party, the Churches of Christ, the quality of religious sectarianism is great—little cooperation with other Christian bodies—but concerning themselves with the faithfulness of others is a recessive matter. Moreover their sense of alienation from the general culture is usually slight. Churches of Christ are Fundamentalist in church but not in attitude towards society. Its members often practice compartmentalization.

In sum, variety characterizes Truth party Evangelicals, the Christians called Fundamentalists. These differ: (1) in spirit, from harsh and judgmental, to aggressive and sarcastic, to self-contained and single-minded; (2) in relation to the society, from negative and condemnatory, to transformative, to ecclesiastically sectarian; (3) on the status of theology, from attention to doctrines, to doctrines and social morality, to texts and church organizational practices.

These Truth-party Christians, though diverse, hold some positions in common. First, they are consistently rationalist in epistemology. The revealed truth of God is regarded as more fundamental than spiritual experience. Assent to doctrines rates higher than a personal relationship of trust. "Experience" lacks the requisite firmness and easily shades off into a dreaded subjectivism that easily corrupts one into relativism.

Second, all live by a conviction that the standard Christian response is obedience, compliance, conformity, and responsibility. Christians are people properly under authority, with orders. They owe obligation to a norm.

Third, a critical stance toward culture is characteristic. While many in the Churches of Christ may practice compartmentalization, participating easily in general society while holding to a quite exclusivist ecclesiology, most Fundamentalists are sectarian and condemnatory toward human culture.

Fourth, and most basic, Fundamentalists—and with a different spirit Evangelicals in general—work from and refer everything to a first principle, an authority. The "principle of principle" underlies Fundamentalist identity, which can only be described as authoritarian. But that is so because its foundation is authority and its mentality authority-mindedness.

Let us endeavor to keep our bearings. All Fundamentalists are Evangelicals. Most Evangelicals are not Fundamentalists. In the South, a minority, actually a rather small minority are Fundamentalists. And the same is true for the nation at large. There is a variety within the Truth party of Evangelical Christians. Some of them warrant classification as Fundamentalist only when care is taken to spell out wherein they are and why they are not neatly so. Notably, the Churches of Christ are more separatist and exclusivist about church life than they are judgmental and hostile toward other Christians and toward human culture and society.

Most southern Christians are Evangelicals; that is to say, they are neither mainline Protestants nor Fundamentalists. That description includes nearly all Southern Baptists, many Methodists, some Presbyterians, and virtually all Assemblies of God and Church of God people—also most black Protestants, whether National Baptist Convention, Inc., NBC "unincorporated," the Progressive National Baptist Convention, the African Methodist Episcopal Church, the AME, Zion, Church, the Christian Methodist Church, and the Church of God in Christ. (We must note, however, that the major black Baptist and Methodist bodies belong to the National Council of Churches.)

Since these denominations and other related ones make up the heavy majority of the southern Christian population, Evangelicalism is powerfully dominant in the region. Only in the South is that party of Christianity so influential—to the point of being normative, the standard by which the meaning of the Christian faith is measured. Thus, in the South the center of gravity is left of center on the historical Christian spectrum, on the radical, Immediatist side, rather than near the middle or to the right on the traditionalist or conservative side. Moreover, the span is fairly narrow.

Of course the Evangelical outlook turns up among other Christian bodies in the South, in places not suitably called "Evangelical" and emphatically not "Fundamentalist." Among Episcopalians, Roman Catholics, and Presbyterians, "charismatic", that is, spirit-filled, demonstrative expressions of deep personal faith, Christianity sometimes appears. The emergence of these forms in traditionally less expressive denominations is more a part of a national surge than a result of southern Evangelicalism's overflowing its banks, however. In fact, Fundamentalism typically and Evangelicalism often view that charismatic movement with alarm, regarding it as dangerous or perhaps heretical. It flirts with the subjectivist-relativist propensity so much feared by the authority-minded rationalists.

Next it is important to emphasize that "reading the Bible literally" is not what distinguishes Fundamentalist versions of Christianity from others. Nor, for that matter, does that feature set apart Evangelicalism generally from other types of Christianity. In the South, to be sure, most doubt that you can take the Bible faithfully and seriously without taking it literally. My observation is, however, that few lay Christians anywhere in this country read or teach the Bible in line with the hermeneutical and critical principles taught to ministers in most seminaries. (And "most" includes not only the "mainline" denominations but also the seminaries of the Southern Baptist Convention and, to a lesser degree, other more sectarian bodies). The seminaries of the United Methodist Church, as a matter of fact, are in the forefront of modern biblical scholarship.

The great majority of southern Evangelicals take the Bible literally. But, by contrast with a major aspect of Evangelical theology in "the North," most of them do not associate it with the defense of its authority. Being less rationalist and with a smaller concern for apologetics than their northern fellow Evangelicals, they are more likely to take its authoritative status for granted than to argue for it. Their use of it focuses on devotional strength, moral guidance, and witnessing to others who need personal salvation.

It is not biblical literalism that distinguishes Fundamentalists or even Evangelicals generally. Many others are biblical literalists—whether by training and intention or by default. The distinguishing mark of classic Evangelicalism—popular southern versions less so—is a preoccupation with authority. The centrality of the Bible's message is magnified as the sole and sufficient standard of faith. But more than that, certain views of the nature of biblical authority are espoused—it is inspired, infallible, and inerrant, as are certain doctrines. Fundamentalism goes beyond most Evangelical teaching. In that camp, not the principle of authority alone is held up but also specific authoritative teachings, with those defined and presented in an authoritarian manner.

Fundamentalist Christians operate with a creedalistic mentality even though they do not honor a particular creed. A set list of doctrines exists and subscription (intellectual assent) to all the items on the list is required, indeed made a test of faith.

As we have noted, for many Fundamentalists what other (self-proclaimed) Christians teach and preach is seen as their business. Scrutiny of others' preachments and exposure of error make up part of their calling. Their attitudes toward mainline churches, most other Evangelicals, and even some other Fundamentalists go beyond refusal to cooperate with them and respect them. Such pure Christians are under divine responsibility to brand these others publicly as apostate. To cite some examples, Bob Jones denounces Billy Graham as a liberal. Bob Jones and Carl McIntyre have barely been on speaking terms for years, though their common opposition to Jerry Falwell has lately brought about some communication between them. Much Fundamentalism is militant in such ways as these. This is not merely a vigorous explicitness about its own convictions and positions but also a strident denunciation about the falsity and perversity of other positions. Fundamentalist militancy has both a positive and negative side.

Underlying this militant sense of authority, certainty, and urgent mission is a world-view, a metaphysic with an attendant epistemology. Quite to the point, Fundamentalism posits a definitive understanding of the relation between the Natural and the Supernatural, the Created Order and the Creator. For Evangelicals generally and Fundamentalists to a heightened degree, one item (or a few items) in the Created Order is an extension of God's reality, thus is exempt from its creaturely status. Or, more accurately in the case of most non-Fundamentalist Evangelicals, any such item transcends its creaturely status. The Bible is the premier instance. But particular doctrines formulated in specified ways may also quality; similarly, for some the conversion experience, for some others the pentecostal experience. The process by which the Bible came to be written is a different kind of example, as is the humanity of the God-Man, Jesus Christ.

What is the role, the standing, the capacity of the Natural Order, of Creation; that is, of things, people, and events? Does the Created Order have any degree of independence from the Creator? How is it used by him as a channel of revelation? Does God overwhelm creation? Or, does he work through it subtly so that only those see who are given eyes of faith to see? (This is the mainline position.) To this series of apposite questions, so fundamental to the understanding of the conservative Christians bent on proclaiming the fundamentals, much sure knowledge is available, thanks to the "no uncertain sound" of God's propositional revelation. Fundamentalists know a great deal and they know for sure. "Perfect" and "pure" are valid categories in their eyes for capturing the texture of revelation. Others may see through a glass darkly, with irony and ambiguity a part of the knowing process, but not Fundamentalists. "Awe" is not a favorite mode of response, nor is "trust." Instead: we know for certain.

This may be a good point at which to sharpen the distinction between Fundamentalist and non-Fundamentalist Evangelicals. As a lot, Evangelical Christians "know" a great deal. They all are confident that God has made an exact and precise, as well as full, disclosure of Himself. But the classic Christian quality of awe is precious and consistently practiced by the non-Fundamentalists. We draw close to the divergence of the two companies when we hear the famous gospel song artist, George Beverly Shea, sing, "Why Should

He Love Me So?'' All Evangelicals might be equally militant—also sectarian and exclusivist—if they all limited their attention to the substance of the revelation, the perfect Bible and absolutely correct doctrines. But non-Fundamentalist Evangelicals probe beneath content to the God of love who made and makes disclosure of Himself. They are thus much taken with the themes of love, grace, and God's spirit, and with the attitudes bound up with those ''soft'' traits of the Lord.

As far as particular beliefs are concerned, the difference between Fundamentalists and other Evangelicals is quantitative. The latter are less likely to measure directly a person's spiritual condition by acts of testing and proving. They also weave together the ''soft'' attitudes just mentioned with firm convictions about strictly held teachings. But, point for point, the two groups diverge in degree only. Similarly, with regard to depth of certainty and commitment and to explicitness of testimony, neither yields any ground to the other. But, finally, the distinctions in attitude or spirit make the difference qualitative. For Fundamentalists, TRUTH outranks everything else. The ministry to truth takes precedence over the ministry to persons. For other Evangelicals, truth and persons tend to be correlated dialectically. That is, as important as the Truth is to them, they acknowledge that the Truth exists in order that people may be served. One finally infers that for the Fundamentalists, Truth has a self-contained status which would make its existence necessary even if there were no people. To paraphrase, the Bible was not made for people, but people were made for the Bible.

In noting that Fundamentalism orders truth ahead of persons, we put a finger, one finger, on the reasons for which that movement has been relatively unattractive to southern people. Some may term it a matter of manners, of ''southern hospitality,'' or the attitude of neighborliness; or something else. It is the case that most southern Evangelicals live with a clear sense of religious authority, of being obligated to the mandates of Holy Scripture. Yet it is probably not accurate to describe them as authority-preoccupied, not even authority-minded. Instead, typically, they are concerned with both truth and persons, correlating the two ministries dialectically. For one thing, theology is less important to most southern Evangelicals than it is to Fundamentalists. Definition, defense, formulation, and argumentation are less endemic than personal piety and churchly mission to the unsaved. For another, they usually view doctrine as having to do with people. It is more a dynamic to be applied than an abstraction to be pronounced. The ingredience of *persons* in the dialectical pair gives practical direction to *truth*; the ingredience of *truth* in the pairing provides clear identify for *persons* together with an urgent sense of mission.

Southerners have done a ''lot of living.'' Theirs is a rather earthy, everyday approach that deals with stresses and celebrates good things. Their characteristic understanding of the Christian Faith has a certain softness about it. This mood and tone are markedly divergent from the abstractness, militancy, and exclusiveness that accompany the Fundamentalist message and practice.

Most southern Christians are high-intensity Evangelicals. Or at least that is the model held up for them and enjoined upon them. But most are not Fundamentalist.

II. HOW IS SOUTHERN RELIGION FUNDAMENTALIST?

Fundamentalism is stronger in the South in the 1980s than it ever began to be in the heyday of American Fundamentalism during the 1920s. Its strength today may be seen in several different expressions of Fundamentalist substance and spirit.

Its most conspicuous manifestation has occurred within the Southern Baptist Convention. Consistently conservative and Evangelical (mostly in a revivalistic way), that denomination has sometimes tolerated and often favored a moderate and diversity-respecting course. However in the late 1970s, a coalition of Fundamentalists organized to take control of the Convention's major offices thereby to determine who would sit on the boards and committees of its agencies and institutions. They have been impressively successful. The consequences add up to a deeply divided body that some observers predict will splinter into two or more organized factions. At any rate the coming to power of a Fundamentalist segment is altering the nature and orientation of the 14.3 million member denomination known historically for a capacity to weather storms. That resiliency has been anchored in its sense of destiny, a factor that is both healthy and pernicious, and the vigorous institutional loyalty it commands.

But other forms too are present in the South. Militant Fundamentalism of the Bob Jones University variety has had a small but visible presence since the 1920s. The independent church movement has gained strength within the past 25 years. These are often Baptist but may fly under other flags or simply describe themselves as "Christian" or "Bible churches" or "full gospel." Some in this movement have loose affiliation with the Baptist Bible Fellowship which has headquarters and a college in Springfield, Missouri. Stemming from the leadership of J. Frank Norris in the 1920s and concentrated in the southwest, it is best known now through the fame of Jerry Falwell and his Thomas Road Baptist congregation in Lynchburg, Virginia. Other large independent congregations are located throughout the South, most of them founded since 1960 and still led by the founding pastor. It is thus too early to assess their long-term roles and lasting influence. Frequently "Christian schools" are supported by these independent churches. Their number and size are growing, thus they give signs of extending Fundamentalist impact far more broadly than the South has felt it in the past. The two Landmark Baptist bodies, the American Baptist Association and the Baptist Missionary Association of America are strong in the Southwest, each claiming 225,000 members.

Something of the same set of concerns has brought into existence the Presbyterian Church in America. It too holds a firm line against modernism and liberal thought, seeking to defend the classic faith of the Reformed tradition against any and all forms of erosion and compromise. Yet the PCA is notably different from other hyperconservative brands of southern Protestantism. For one thing its rationalism and scholasticism are rooted in a long and highly developed Calvinist theological tradition. For another, its constituency is solidly middle and upper class people whose posture is not sectarian or hostile to culture. Being right is more important to the PCA than being different.

Examination of historical context is needed at this point, of some southern history, also some northern, and considerable comparative American history. Around 1900 in the South, a clash occurred over religion. Dissent and conflict were emerging, especially within the Methodist and the Baptist ranks. The importance of this eruption was by contrast with a relatively peaceful nineteenth century religious scene when most had been defenders of the old order. In the words of David Edwin Harrell, Jr.;

> It had not always been so. In the nineteenth century religious radicalism flourished mostly in other sections of the nation. The great revivals of the pre-Civil War period were primarily western and northern and the most important new nineteenth-century sects, the Disciples of Christ, Mormons, adventists, and holiness, were clearly products of those regions. Southerners were proud that their religion had remained more traditional. In 1833, one southern minister boasted: "Mormonism, adventism, sanctificationism, spiritualism, woman's rights, free love, and all such, started north of the Mason and Dixon's line."
>
> The South's avoidance of sectarianism in the nineteenth century highlighted the region's religious uniformity in the midst of a century of change.[3]

These sectarian disturbances around 1900, disrupting a hitherto calm picture, were serious and their results lasting. But we must see these developments for what they were. Class conflict was basic, reflecting the yearning of the poor and the dispossessed (mostly white people) for religious communities and styles of their own—at a time when the traditional denominations were becoming highly organized and more "progressive." Also, we must note that the appearance of the various Pentecostal and Holiness bodies

---

[3]David Edwin Harrell, Jr., *Varieties of Southern Evangelicalism* (Macon, Ga.: Mercer University Press, 1981) 47.

did not result from bitter clashes on the floor or denominational conventions. They occurred through local departures and formations, not as a result of official confrontation.

In the North, religious conflict was heating up from the 1880s to reach fever pitch in the 1920s. There a clash of cultures was occurring, a head-on conflict over ideas. Battle lines arrayed ''Modernists'' against ''Fundamentalists'' in the struggle between those who would adapt and those who would entrench. Denominational conventions sometimes turned into donnybrooks. New bodies came into being, the Orthodox Presbyterian, the Bible Presbyterian, and the General Association of Regular Baptists, for example; a company of conservatives who remained Northern Baptists founded three seminaries to accord with their theological tastes.

Up north, the conflict hinged around several issues: social concerns and ministries versus evangelism and missions; modes of interpreting Scripture; disagreement over specific doctrines, notably millennialism; denominational integrity over against ecumenism; the relation of science to theism. By and large, those were not the issues claiming the attention of the major southern denominations at the time. Some reverberations were felt in the 1920s, to be sure, over the appearance of the evolutionary view of cosmic origins. With respect to the social sciences, there were few responses to the invasion of naturalistic currents of thought, partly because that invasion was minor. Freud, Comte, and Marx were hardly big news in the South.

Not that all was serene in the southern society of the 1920s. Cries of alarm had been expressed before World War I over the threatened import of alien people and alien ways into an ethnically, religiously, and culturally ''pure'' society. But that was a spectre of trouble not an actual intrusion. There was more xenophobia than actual conflict with enemies on the field. Granted, alternative ways of viewing reality and constructing society appeared here and there. But mostly these were being heard of at a distance, as new trends or fads that had begun to despoil northern society.

The South experienced no fundamental dislocation. Few immigrants moved in. Few urban centers had sprung up. Few significant universities had developed as yet. The process of modernization had begun to creep into southern culture but its implantation was shallow—really up until World War II.

Take the celebrated war of the worlds at Dayton, Tennessee, in the summer of 1925. The future of traditional southern civilization was not at stake in that courthouse contest over the teaching of Darwinian evolution. What really happened at this late date was that public high schools were now functioning in deeply rural areas for the first time and in them biology was being taught by people trained in colleges or universities. In unintended and at first unrecognized ways, occasion for fear had appeared in the South.

In the South of the 1920s, there really were not many subversive causes to oppose; few profound threats to cultural continuity were in evidence. No struggle to the death over eternal verities or over ethnic and cultural purity was gripping the region during this period. Also, down to the Great Depression, a positive program of economic development brought a sense of hope and promise to many in the regional population. The South of the 1920s was relatively prosperous compared to its own past and to many western nations.

Even with the ravages of the Depression painfully in mind, I believe we can make a case for the 1920s and 1930s turning out to be a season of refreshment to southern civilization. The region's storied great literature began to appear, great by universal standards, that is, not regional. It had been a long time since the South had produced a great cultural attainment. As Allen Tate wrote, a whole generation of writers began to look around and see that the Yankees were not to blame for everything that had gone wrong. Diverted from attributing the region's woes to others, the major writers, led by William Faulkner, converted the southern legend into a ''universal myth of the human condition.'' A shift occurred ''from melodramatic rhetoric to the dialectic of tragedy.'' A leading edge of southern society was transcending the province in favor of a comparative perspective.[4]

The collection of essays published as *I'll Take My Stand* is more representative of the southern response to ''a new world a comin' '' than any images of hand to hand mortal conflict resulting from the confrontation of two civilizations. The southern intellectuals who wrote for that 1930 publication were appealing for conservation of a specific sort, the conservation of the values and ways of life of an older society that gave high place to family, community, and agrarian-related virtues. They were not crusading for a South that totally closed its eyes to the currents and developments in ''modern society.'' While strongminded and idealistic, they stopped short of preaching dire warnings of what was about to occur. Both these groups of regional intellectuals aimed to call the South to is own heritage. This positive program, though with some near reactionary representatives, stood as a thoughtful and constructive response to new social conditions, both real and looming. A new order was in the offing and some leaders were envisioning the shape of the future, but no revolution was at hand.

In the major denominations, the 1920s witnessed a scare over evolution. But in the main that decade and the next were a time of growth and uniting. The Southern Baptist Convention began to take on the shapes we associate it with today during that period. It developed and enlarged boards and agencies

---

[4]See Allen Tate, ''A Southern Mode of the Imagination,'' in *Studies in American Culture*, eds. Joseph J. Kwiat and Mary C. Turpie (Minneapolis: University of Minnesota Press, 1960) 96-108.

and hit upon a centralized form of funding that has made it a wealthy and efficient organization. The Methodist Episcopal Church, South, always of two minds about existence in two regional divisions, merged with its northern counterpart in 1939, a reunion producing "The Methodist Church."

Overall, conditions in the South were improving for the churches and for the (white) population. This time of growth and relative health was not matched by the religious situation prevalent in the North. There Fundamentalism, always at least partly a reactionary movement, was erupting in the face of what was perceived as a frontal assault on everything holy and dear. The 1920s were described by concerned Protestant conservatives as an "age of insanity" and a "crisis in common sense."

The South's cultural condition did not throw up menacing forces or movements exciting strident reaction. Evolution was an issue for a time but the massive force called Modernism was not. Hints of the invasion of this enemy appeared, but none threatened to undermine orthodoxy in the churches or take over the culture. Moreover, after 1929 the South was in no position to react. Reaction of this kind is a sort of luxury. The Great Depression struck with full fury preempting any such luxury. There were dangers, all right, but they were deeply practical, food, clothing, housing, jobs, health, and income.

A seeming exception to this interpretation is George Marsden's argument that in the 1920s the centers of American Fundamentalism shifted from the North to the South. The facts are indeed worth noting. As we have seen, Bob Jones planted his college at Cleveland, Tennessee, in 1927. Dallas Theological Seminary was begun in 1924. Its spiritual founder was C. I. Scofield, a Tennesseean who really spent his life in the Midwest. These two institutions have continued to this day as part of the regional landscape. But they are far from prominent in the religious life of the region; in fact in their own locales, they are seen as culturally alien. The conservatism which characterizes the mainline denominations, Baptist, Methodist, and Presbyterian, is a different kind from the Fundamentalism of these two institutions (and their sister schools), and also from the Pentecostal and Holiness orientation of large numbers of Southerners.

As if to highlight the relative scarcity of Fundamentalist forms in the South, not withstanding the alleged shift of the centers from North to South, Marsden writes:

> In the South the debates were in most cases short-lived, because dissent was simply not tolerated. As early as the first half of the nineteenth century, advanced theological views had usually been associated with advanced social views and abolition. Southern theology already had a strong conservative bent. The War Between the States simply intensified Southern determination to resist change. Hence there was a strong anti-modernist impulse in

Southern religion well before modernism became a distinct movement in America. This theological conservatism, often combined with the warm revivalist evangelicalism inherited from the early nineteenth century, created in Southern religion many characteristics that resembled later fundamentalism. Until the 1920s, however, Southern revivalist conservatism and Northern fundamentalism developed more or less independently, although in parallel ways. The principal direct connection between the two movements was that several important fundamentalist leaders came from the South. When in the twentieth century fundamentalism became a distinct entity, Southerners with a long history of revivalist conservatism eventually flocked to the movement.[5]

I regard "flocked to the movement" as somewhat too strong. But Marsden is correct and perceptive in noting that southern conservatism was, *mutatis mutandis*, a kind of Fundamentalism; or, we may conjecture that many Southern Christians might have been Fundamentalists had the external circumstances been ripe for it and their own regional theological traditions more rationalistic.

In the 1920s at least one engagement between northern Fundamentalist thought and southern theology occurred. In Marsden's words:

> The intellectual issue probably was most clearly defined in the thought of J. Gresham Machen, as expressed in his critique of a non-fundamentalist conservative, E. Y. Mullins. Mullins, the distinguished president of Southern Baptist Theological Seminary in Louisville, attempted to bridge the gap between traditional and modern thought in his own defense of supernatural Christianity, published in 1924 as *Christianity at the Cross Roads*. Machen reviewed this work of 'a true friend,' but took the opportunity to expound his belief that the compromises which Mullins allowed would eventually result in the destruction of Christianity.
>
> Mullins had attempted to save supernatural Christianity from the depredations of modern science by arguing that religion should be held separate from both philosophy and science. Religion, he said, was not governed by the principles of science and philosophy, but rather by its own principle of "personal relation." Such a relation could be confirmed only by "the immediate experience of God."
>
> Machen replied that science, philosophy, and religion all dealt with precisely the same thing—facts. Either persons saw the facts correctly or they did not. Hence, contrary to Mullins's view only one philosophy could be true. False science and philosophy resulted when sin obscured the facts or led one to accept naturalistic presuppositions that excluded some of the facts. So, said Machen, 'We ought to try to lead scientists and philosophers to become Christians not by asking them to regard science and philosophy

---

[5]*Fundamentalism and American Culture* 103.

as without bearing upon religion, but on the contrary by asking them to become more scientific and more philosophical through attention to all, instead of to some, of the facts.'

Machen regarded Mullins's position as a dangerous concession in principle to the chief tendency in modern thought—away from direct knowledge of facts to subjective experience. The issue was most clear with respect
to the resurrection of Jesus. According to the assumptions of modern thought,
Machen pointed out, scientific history could only talk about 'the belief of
the disciples in the resurrection.' Machen, on the other hand, in accordance
with Common Sense Realism assumed that what we know about in history
is not the *idea* of the event (which is in the present) but the event itself (which
is in the past). It would not do to say, as Mullins did, that religion dealt with
'spirit' rather than with 'matter.' 'The question of the resurrection of our
Lord,' said Machen, 'in accordance with the common-sense definition of
''resurrection'' ' which Dr. Mullins certainly holds, does concern ''matter''; it concerns the emergence or non-emergence of the ideas about the
event; ultimately it came down to 'whether the event really took place.'[6]

Earlier reference has been made to millennialism, a doctrine in Christian
theology that is prominent in Fundamentalist thought but rarely a central article in the southern creed. In dealing with when Christ's Second Coming will
occur, before or after a divinely-planned thousand year period, millennialism
implies a philosophy of history called dispensationalism. Looking at history
in a dispensationalist way is the ultimate in rationalism, in subjecting the entire historical process to a precise classification. It is an ''anti-developmental
and anti-naturalistic way of explaining historical change.''[7] It sponsors a
heightened supernaturalism. In dispensationalist thought, ''Human efforts and
natural forces have almost nothing to do with historical change.[8]''

It is important to mention millennialism and dispensationalism in this paper on Fundamentalism and the South for the sake of showing how slightly
they have converged, until the past decade or so. The kind of rationalism that
informs those theological positions is largely foreign to southern sensibilities. Southerners have been more eager to spread faith than to defend the faith.
This choice is due partly to the nature of revivalism and partly to the lack of
enemies against whom to construct a defense. Fundamentalism requires a
worked out rational structure. By contrast, popular southern modalities *feel*
religion more than they *think* about it. As for the use of Scripture, it is more
common to deal with verses than with systematic theology or comprehensive
themes, and to take its authoritative status for granted than to make the case
for that status.

---

[6]*Fundamentalism and American Culture* 216.
[7]Ibid., 230.
[8]Ibid., 321.

Concerning the classification of history into (the seven) dispensations, maybe the travail of southern history disinclined Southerners from abstract or even supernaturalistic theories of history. The tensions of the antebellum period were followed by the destructiveness of the Civil War which were succeeded by the social ravages of Reconstruction and its aftermath. To be sure, Southerners saw history providentially, including their own sometimes tragic history, but along earthy and existential lines.

Millennialism and dispensationalism are, further, world-denying, while southern religion (and views of living generally) is world-affirming. It is too much at home in its culture to look above and beyond it to see what God is doing. Some millennialism may be found; there have been some currents of it since the 1920s. But when a mainstream Southerner runs into it, it strikes him as a departure from what he is accustomed to. A church that describes itself as ''independent-fundamental-premillennial'' on its bulletin board thereby gives away its eccentric orientation. Many such churches are to be found in the South, but they are ''off-brand'' or for people of limited means and intelligence.

To this point, much has been said about white Southerners and their religion and little about black Southerners. That is because Fundamentalism has been almost totally absent from black religion. Evangelical it is, but not Fundamentalist. At the heart of the matter, rationalism is not a common epistemic mode in black religion. Some superficial observations might attribute the absence of rationalism to the historically low levels of education in the American black community. But that is simply irrelevant (never mind whether it is true) since rationalist epistemology is not a function of education or intelligence, high or low (indeed no epistemic mode is so correlated). Rationalism is, after all, no more than a viewpoint, a way of knowing, a means of conceiving of the nature of things.

Among blacks in the South the experience of life and of its transcendent dimensions has been rooted in slavery and segregation, that is, travail, oppression, and deprivation. That set of conditions has surely contributed to (though hardly determined) an existential, intuitionist, rational mode of knowing. Blacks have done a great deal of reflecting on life, its meaning, and the course of events. Religiously, that has issued in calling out to a personal God seen as participating in the affairs of their history to deliver them from their oppressive circumstances. Deliverance is indeed a central theme for black Christians. Associated with it is an expressive response of joy and celebration. Foreign to it is scrupulosity of belief and creating checks for orthodoxy. To be sure the Christianity of black Americans is orthodox. But it is an orthodoxy to which churches relate easily and comfortably and it is a standard based on traditional biblical preaching rather than a theology to be measured against a creedal tradition. Furthermore, the doctrinal positions of black

churches are always correlated with and tempered by the centrality of vital
worship and by a vigorous communal ethic.

This *modus operandi* is continuous with patterns that emerged in the early
decades of the independent black denominations. A recent study of ministers
in the black church from 1856-1902 by Edward L. Wheeler makes the point
forcefully:

> . . . the elite clergy . . . stood within the mainstream of American, and to
> some extent, even southern Protestantism. Yet that theology also addressed
> the particular needs of a people trying to etch out a niche for themselves in
> American society. Precisely because of its combination of seemingly dis-
> tinctive motifs—an otherworldly traditional theology and a theology of so-
> cial change—it could provide for black people a sense of their own value
> and worth. It permitted them to hold to the piety of their childhood while
> yet moving beyond it. It offered reaffirmation in the face of a hostile white
> society's denial of their humanity. The notions of the fatherhood of God and
> brotherhood of man provided hope for uplifting the race.[9]

The absence of Fundamentalism from the black church in the South is
highly significant for the incidence of Fundamentalism in the South generally. It means that at least 20% of the southern population is largely unaf-
fected by Fundamentalist Christianity, with implications for the entire culture.
Black Christians' vital role in the culture has contributed to religion's re-
maining more practical and experimental than abstract and rational.

Earlier I remarked that Fundamentalism is stronger in the South today than
it ever was in the heyday of Fundamentalism in the North. But we also noted
the presence of forms of that "patchwork coalition," namely, the independent churches (often Baptist), the archconservatives within the Southern
Baptist Convention, and the continuation of such centers of influence as the
Bob Jones orbit, Dallas Theological Seminary, the Southwide Baptist Fellowship, and others.

But the conspicuous manifestation of Fundamentalism is the person and
influence of Jerry Falwell, especially through the Liberty Federation (or Moral
Majority, Inc.), the political arm of his ministry. It is important to recognize
that the South is neither the heartland of this movement nor a society over-
whelmed by it. Its response to the New Christian Right is complex, as James
L. Guth's research on Southern Baptist ministers' attitudes attests:

> Although Southern Baptist ministers are deeply ambivalent about organi-
> zations such as Moral Majority, they are clearly in the conservative camp
> on most issues. Still, on some questions a substantial minority with more
> moderate or even liberal views appears. At first glance it might seem this

---

[9]Edward L. Wheeler, *Uplifting the Race: The Black Minister in the New South, 1865-
1902*," (Ph.D. diss. Emory University, 1982).

minority is sure to grow: the ministers are drawn from middle-class backgrounds, have both college and seminary degrees, and serve the burgeoning middle-class, urban contingent within the SBC. The increasing numbers of such ministers and congregations would seem to provide the basis for a strong moderate-to-liberal faction.

However, there are clear countervailing tendencies. The shift in the Southern Baptist center of gravity from the South Atlantic states to the Deep South and Southwest continues and will strengthen the hand of conservatives. In a related vein, conservative seminaries in the same regions have grown most rapidly, producing added numbers of ministerial conservatives. And new ministers everywhere are predominantly conservative, augmenting the potential for Christian Right politics. These conflicting forces, combined with increased activism by the most conservative and the most liberal ministers alike, point toward increasing politicization and polarization within the denomination. Thus the Southern Baptist Convention, like the South itself, may be seeing the rise of two-party politics. The battles of the past few years may just be skirmishes preliminary to a much longer war.[10]

We must reiterate that while the New Christian Right shows some southern flavor and is popularly identified with southern religious ways, it is a national, not a regional, movement both in its concerns and in its constituency. Some of the leadership is being provided by the South, most notably Falwell's but his viewers are far from typically southern. And the following that he has attracted is not conspicuously regional.

What we are witnessing on the religious-political front is a several-layered response to conditions in America over the past 30 and more years: the liberalism and excessivism of the 1960s; the secularization of American society; and (what is perceived as) the erosion of traditional values. The South participates in that—perhaps more as a culture that believes it has resources for combatting those destructive currents than as an as-yet ravaged society. There is no mistaking its having become a part of American society. Some erosion is occurring there too. And the process of secularization is hardly a stranger there. The region is responding to a national condition—sickness, it would be called—and also to the loss of old ways of being southern. One subtle part of the response may be the limited success attained so far in the attempt to build an authentic and concordantly biracial society.

Personally I doubt that Fundamentalism will take over the South. The center of gravity has indeed shifted a bit toward the religious right. But one observer's "educated guess" is that it is likely to go on being a society dominated by Evangelicalism, not one riven and driven by Fundamentalist views of the truth and of a healthy American society.

---

[10]James L. Guth, "Preachers and Politics" in *Religion and Politics in the South*, eds. Tod A. Baker, Robert P. Steed, Laurence W. Moreland (New York: Praeger, 1983) 181.

"COMMONLY, (THOUGH FALSELY) CALLED . . . ": REFLECTIONS ON THE SEARCH FOR BAPTIST IDENTITY

WILLIAM H. BRACKNEY
EASTERN BAPTIST THEOLOGICAL SEMINARY
PHILADELPHIA PA 19151

Some mainstream Baptists in the United States currently have an identity crisis. Faced with declining numbers and changing socio-economic factors, American Baptists in 1984 appointed a blue ribbon national commission of biblical scholars, theologians and historians to establish clearly what [and who] American Baptists are. On another track, an American Baptist program called ''Grow By Caring'' emphasizes the ''mark of identity'' and national program leaders urge local church folk to use ABC curriculum resources and to read the denominational magazine to sharpen the sense of being an American Baptist. Similarly, for about four years now, Southern Baptists have experienced painful dissension over what constitutes a real Southern Baptist—those in the ''New Right'' who are attempting to control SBC machinery, or the more progressive institutional types who operate the seminaries, the regional and national program agencies. Southern Baptists have been urged to affirm the 1963 ''Baptist Faith and Message Statement,'' to reflect on the past heroes and heroines of Southern Baptist life, and above all, to take pride in the ever-

expanding domestic and overseas SBC missionary thrusts.[1] While two major
Baptist groups in America have suffered this identity crisis, smaller, non-
aligned Baptist congregations and bodies have held their own, or grown, and
do not overtly express any such "crisis."

Historian Edwin S. Gaustad has recently observed that "Baptists appear
to have more problems than most as we endeavor to locate that distillation,
that essence, that defining difference which constitutes being Baptist." Baptists have no Canterbury, John Wesley, or 1517 birthdate to which to point
with unquestioned assurance. Moreover, Baptists have a long history of being
deliberately misunderstood in order to be violently attacked," Gaustad points
out.[2] One is left to conclude, therefore, that our identity crisis is not a recent
phenomenon, but a longstanding problem for us and the larger Christian world.

For most Christian groups, identity is achieved by a recognizable historical origin and a continuing differentiation from other groups and ideas which
the adherents positively affirm. Unclear origins suggest diffuse evolution and
organizational discontinuity; continuously evolving polity and piety lead to a
lack of group solidarity and cohesion from one generation to the next. Baptists have been plagued by such realities. The result? An historic identity crisis.

By contrast, in the Methodist tradition, scores of Wesleyan types all claim
John Wesley as a parent and even are willing every hundred years or so to
celebrate with each other.[3] Similarly, Lutherans may divide on issues like
scriptural authority and lifestyle, but all synods plainly and proudly acknowledge St. Martin and their creeds as the core of a tradition.[4] Within the Free
Churches like the Baptists, however, problems arise.

Almost from the beginning, adversaries to the Baptists helped to shape
denominational identity. The epithet "anabaptist" was quickly applied and
as one writer put it, the force of the discredited name alone pulled them down.

---

[1]*American Baptists Grow By Caring: A Manual for Congregational Reflection and Response* (Valley Forge: National Ministries, 1985); *SBC Today: A National Autonomous Publication of News and Opinion for Southern Baptists*: see especially 2:7 (November 1984).

[2]Edwin S. Gaustad, "Toward a Baptist Identity in the Twenty-First Century" in William
H. Brackney, ed., *Discovering Our Baptist Heritage* (Valley Forge: A.B.H.S., 1985) 86-89.

[3]Although great diversity exists among Methodists, including those who emphasize holiness theology and those who stress social action, in 1884 and 1984, the various branches
planned centennial and bicentennial study sessions and celebrations where differences were
laid aside for common heritage. The United Methodists used the opportunity to unveil a new
headquarters for their Commission on Archives and History in Madison, New Jersey.

[4]Similarly, among Lutherans there is a recognition of a common creedal and hymnic tradition which Lutheran historian Martin Marty has observed describes Lutheranism in a special
way. See his *Lutherans and Roman Catholicism: The Changing Conflict 1917-1963* (South
Bend: Notre Dame, 1968).

In public debates such as the famous one held at Southwark in 1642, English Baptists were abusively harrassed by the question, "Are you anabaptists?" Thousands of miles away in Massachusetts Bay Colony in the same era, a law was passed whereby those "who have held the baptizing of infants unlawful" could be banished from the colony altogether.[5] As late as the eighteenth century, John Wesley still referred to this class of nonconformists as "anabaptists," thus continuing the unfair label which by that time was surely inappropriate.

The ways in which Baptists have attempted to cope with their identity crises of the past should serve as a commentary on the present problem. In the seventeenth century, Baptists (both General and Particular) issued formal statements, called confessions, to establish their identity. Between 1800 and 1900, Baptists were identified by what seemed to be a dauntless missionary crusade with a homespun biblicism.[6] Recently, as Baptist groups have proliferated, the whole matter of identity has become less clear and both Baptists and non-Baptists have had a hard time making many generalizations. To deal with the problem, contemporary voices have proposed several bold solutions like reducing many Baptist distinctives to the lowest common denominators, articulating a clear Baptist theology and establishing commissions to give verbal shape to a denominational body. In light of Baptist history, two of these approaches are problematic, while the other has possibilities.

THE PROBLEM WITH ISOLATING KEY BAPTIST EMPHASES

Prior to the early nineteenth century, Baptists in America understood who they were as did their adversaries. A demand for believers' baptism and congregational independence usually separated Baptists from other Christians as Baptists held tenaciously to these points. However, with the advent of voluntary benevolent societies, a rift occurred among the churches and associations which called into question within the denomination itself what constituted a Baptist. The leaders of the Triennial Convention were sure that such extra-church organizations would advance Baptist principles—Richard Furman, its first president, exulted in an address, "We *have* one Lord, one faith, one baptism . . . "[7] But to an equal degree, local church protectionists, in some regions called the anti-mission movement, opposed such organiza-

---

[5]The law is found in *The Book of the General Laws and Libertyes Concerning the Inhabitants of the Massachusetts Bay Colony* (Cambridge: Green, 1648) 1.

[6]The story is ably told in Robert G. Torbet, *Venture of Faith: The Story of the American Baptist Foreign Mission Society 1814-1854* (Valley Forge: Judson Press, 1955).

[7]*Proceedings of the First Triennial Meeting of the General Missionary Convention*, May 1814 6.

tion as foreign to the spirit of Baptists, and they considered such principles as a subversion of the order marked out in the New Testament.[8]

For the mainstream churches, the American Baptist Publication Society created a series of tracts and pamphlets which sought to define historic Baptist emphases or principles. These included ''Practical Uses of Baptism,'' ''Moral Dignity of Missionary Enterprise,'' ''Duties of Church Members Towards Each Other,'' and ''Terms of Communion.'' Often such literature allowed for increased cooperation among churches and broader interpretations of church membership, the Lord's Supper and ordination, just to mention some of the key issues. A tradition of strict adherence to less compromising standards began in the anti-missionary movement and reached its fullest expression in the Landmarkist literature, beginning about 1850. Landmarkers like James R. Graves and James M. Pendleton carefully listed Baptist emphases which they called the ''landmarks of the fathers'' and called upon all true Baptists to adhere to their historic principles. Graves' list included a local rather than a universal church and an entirely regenerate congregation; believers' baptism by immersion and closed communion were the only ordinances of gospel churches.[9]

The net effect of listing Baptist emphases was to promote a test among many in the denomination to establish a Baptist purity. This trend was certainly evident in the early Modernist-Fundamentalist battles of the twentieth century, when, especially among both Northern and Southern Baptists, Fundamentalists listed historic Baptist principles (including specific positions on the origins of Scripture) and called upon the denomination to discipline those who disagreed. Virtually all of the dissenter groups which left either the Northern or Southern Conventions adopted confessional statements which clearly specified Baptist fundamentals.[10] In response, The Northern Convention chose to emphasize religious liberty and doctrinal pluralism and in 1963 the Southern Convention adopted the moderate ''Baptist Faith and Message Statement'' which was said to be a set of guidelines of ''things surely believed,'' but not an official creed and carrying no mandatory authority.[11]

Recently, the suggestion to codify Baptist emphases has again emerged. James McClendon argues that certain ''baptist'' marks—biblicism, mission,

---

[8]*Proceedings Drafted by the Particular Baptists Convened at Black Rock, Maryland on September 28, 1832*, 14. The ''Black Rock Resolutions'' were considered the classic statement of the antimissionary forces in the East.

[9]James R. Graves, *Old Landmarkism: What Is it?* (Nashville: Baptist Book House, 1880) 131-41.

[10]Many of these statements are found in William L. Lumpkin, *Baptist Confessions of Faith* (Philadelphia: Judson Press, 1959).

[11]The statement was printed for mass distribution in 1964 under the title ''The Baptist Faith and Message.''

liberty, discipleship and community—are characteristic of all the believers'
churches, Anabaptist as well as Baptist.[12] While this theologian revives an
age-old possibility of Baptist relationships with the heirs of the Radical Reformation, his marks are too blurry to please either liberal or strict ''capital
B'' baptists, who in one case are more interested in historical accuracy, and
in the other instance, want more doctrinal purity than McClendon offers.

A major difficulty in any list of Baptist emphases or distinguishing marks
is the diversity now existing among Baptists. A profile which may legiti-
mately delineate the character of one group, say the Italian Baptist Association, by no means fits the General Association of Regular Baptists. The
doctrinal principles of the Baptist Bible Fellowship will probably never be
acceptable to the American Baptist Churches in the USA, and so forth. Lists
of emphases, self-created to distinguish one group, cannot be ultimately and
generally useful in establishing a positive overall Baptist identity. More often
than not, such lists become tools of negative sanction.

THE PROBLEM OF A UNIQUELY BAPTIST THEOLOGY

Some writers are convinced that an important approach to Baptist identity
is to articulate a Baptist theology which follows in the train of an historically
unique theological tradition. As one teacher has put it, ''Baptists do have a
theology. We have always had one and we are going to go on having one!''[13]
But, is there any credibility in such overstatement?

If Baptist theology means the existence of Baptists who have produced
serious theological literature, there is ample evidence. From the earliest years
of the seventeenth century, there is a rich heritage of Baptist inspired theological writings. This heritage includes John Smyth's *Differences in the
Churches of the Separation* (1608), numerous confessions of faith, and apol-
ogetic materials usually focused upon baptism, like the Englishman, Samuel
Fisher's *Baby-Baptism, Mere Babism* (1653). The greatest accomplishments
of early Baptist theological expression are Thomas Grantham's *Christianismus Primitivus* (1678) and of course, John Gill's *Body of Doctrinal Divinity*
(1769). These last two works compare easily and forcefully with similar Prot-

---

[12]James W. McClendon, Jr., *Systematic Theology: Ethics* (New York: Abingdon, 1986)
27-37, discusses at length his thesis concerning a ''baptist'' theology which he identifies with
historically Anabaptist and Baptist groups. Unfortunately, he does not exhibit a clear perception of the documented historical realities in the independent evolutions of these Christian traditions and consequently, the unique social and religious contexts for their theologies. His
decapitalization of ''Baptist'' is a unique approach.

[13]George Peck, ''Baptists and Their Theology: Toward a New Appreciation,'' paper presented at The American Baptist Faculty Consultation, 24-26 February 1984, 2.

estant theologies of the period, and, as Gill's work reflects, later editions were popular well into the nineteenth century.[14]

During the period when William Paley, Adam Clarke, and Nathaniel W. Taylor were producing major theological traditions in other denominations, Baptists were content mostly with practical theological tracts devoted to specific subject matter such as the ordinances, evangelism and missions. The leading exception was the work of Francis Wayland who, largely an ethicist, profoundly affected American Protestant thought and Baptist polity with his *Elements of Moral Science* (1835) and *Notes on the Principles and Practices of Baptist Churches* (1858).

The later nineteenth century saw a flowering of Baptists who published systematic theologies. The majority of such folk were professors in theological schools whose books reflected published versions of lecture notes: John L. Dagg (1857), John J. Butler (1861), G. D. Pepper (1873), Alvah Hovey (1877), Augustus H. Strong (1886), William N. Clarke (1874), Ezekiel G. Robinson (1894), E. Y. Mullins (1917) and Walter Rauschenbusch (1917). Most of these works were popular at least within the theological schools, with Strong, Clarke and Rauschenbusch achieving reputations within the larger Christian tradition.

As the categories of Baptists have increased in the twentieth century, so also have the shades of theological opinion and the attendant literature. For instance, among the conservatives and moderates there are W. T. Conner (1936), Carl F. Henry (1958), Bernard Ramm (1966), and Dale Moody (1981). More liberal thinkers include Milton Evans (1900), Shailer Mathews (1924), Harvey Cox (1965), and William Hamilton (1966).

Such an impressive list of theological accomplishments belies a recent comment that "there are few Baptist theologians of merit."[15] However, the real question about our list of theologians is, "What can be identified as uniquely Baptist?" Can we assume the rather myopic perspective that merely being a Baptist produces a wholistic world view which can be rationalized in systematic theological pronouncements? Such a perspective does disservice both to Baptist theologians and to our dependence upon Protestant and historically Christian theology.

---

[14]Thomas Grantham, *Christianismus Primitivus: or the Ancient Christian Religion, in its nature, certainty, excellency, and beauty . . .* (London: Smith, 1678); John Gill, *A Body Of Doctrinal Divinity* (London: n.p., 1768). As recently as 1985 an American edition was available from The Baptist Book Trust.

[15]McClendon, *Systematic Theology* 21, does discuss eight "baptist"/Baptist theologians, but neglects many others. Of his list, Roger Williams, John Leland and Isaac Backus are dubious as Baptist *theologians* of the earlier contexts; but also Augustus Strong and William N. Clarke are mistakenly categorized as part of the context of "The Modernist-Fundamentalist Controversy" 31.

The early Baptist theological writings reveal deliberate dependence upon Protestant (particularly Puritan/Separatist) and perhaps Anabaptist literature. John Smyth's Confession of 1610 was an attempt to demonstrate the similarity of a small group of Baptists with the Waterlander Mennonites. The Second London Confession of 1677 was designed to "manifest consent with fundamental articles of the Christian faith . . . and Protestants in diverse actions and cities"[16] and Thomas Grantham in 1678 plainly recognized his dependence upon "founders, advancers continuers and obstructors" of Christianity.[17] John Gill prefaced his magnum opus by recognizing that "since the Reformation we have had bodies or systems of Divinity which have been very serviceable to lead men into the knowledge of evangelical doctrine," which Gill enriched with a greater appreciation for the primitive church. The principal point of departure in each case which may be identified as uniquely Baptist, was the treatment of the church and the ordinances. The church as "a company of visible saints called and separated from the world . . . and baptized into that faith" set the early Baptists apart theologically.[18]

In the eighteenth and early nineteenth centuries, the Baptist ecclesiology and emphasis upon the proper administration of the ordinances often created unnecessary antagonism between Baptists and other Christians in theological discussions. There were few, if any, debates about Scripture, tradition, or Christian experience between Baptists and others; instead, Baptists busied themselves trying to convince the public that they were closest to the primitive churches in composition and practice. A change in this trend occurred as Baptist theological school teachers began to publish their theologies. Strong and Clarke revealed their dependence upon American Reformed theologians, while Mullins and Rauschenbusch evinced an influence from European thought. The broadening educational community of Baptists in the last two decades of the nineteenth century demanded dialogue with Baptists in Europe and within the United States and even between Baptists and other Christian groups.[19] Sadly for the majority of Baptists, however, most Baptist clergy were self-educated and did not enjoy the benefits of progressive theological dis-

---

[16]*Confession of Faith Put Forth by the Elders and Brethren of Many Congregations of Christians* . . . (London: 1677) 244-45.

[17]Grantham, *Christianismus Primitivus* vi.

[18]Gill, *Body of Dictrinal Divinity* 21; art. xxxiii, *The Confession of Faith of those Churches Which Are Commonly (though falsely) Called Anabaptists* (London: Simmons, 1644).

[19]See for example the *Proceedings of the Baptist Congress*, 1880-1900, where Baptist theologians from the United States and Europe gathered frequently to exchange papers and reviews. Further, the work of D. C. MacIntosh at Yale Divinity School won wide acceptance among non-Baptists in the U.S. and Canada. On MacIntosh, see S. Mark Heim, "The Path of a Liberal Pilgrim: A Theological Biography of Douglas Clyde MacIntosh", *American Baptist Quarterly* 4:3 (September 1985): 300-19.

cussion. Indeed, it is probably fair to say that most Baptists lacked any systematic theological understanding and preferred to deal with matters of evangelism and church discipline.

At present, the divisions between so-called liberals and so-called conservatives within the Baptist family present a formidable obstacle to a Baptist theological consensus. One of the historic functions of theology among Baptists has been to protect certain traditions, which often prevents creative discussion and the formulation of new ideas. An example of this is the overwhelming amount of treatment given to scriptural origins questions among conservatives, who still disregard historical biblical scholarship in large measure. Conversely, those in the liberal tradition appear to have little interest in apologetics and busy themselves with "single issue" theological reflection on themes such as social justice and world order.[20]

Finally, Baptists like other Protestants, have become much more eclectic in their recent theological menus. The principal dialogues are not among Baptists, but between Baptists and both Protestants and Catholics. Many in the conservative tradition have adopted a dispensational or an old-Princetonian theological approach while one is likely to hear more liberal Baptists speak supportively of Hans Küng, Harold O. J. Brown or John Cobb. Both polarities appear to be fascinated with Barthian and Brunnerian schools which recognizably changed the theological landscape earlier in this century. Indeed, feminist voices are now being heard among Baptist theologians who question whether systematic theology is desirable any longer, citing its earlier paternalistic and archaic philosophical foundations.[21]

A disjunctive denominational history has had its toll. There appears to be little chance that a Baptist identity will be forged from present theological trends.

A CONCILIAR APPROACH

At first glance, this appears to be problematic in the Free Church tradition, yet at least two major Baptist groups are already moving in this direc-

---

[20]Typical of the conservative approach and interest is Robert P. Lightner, *The Saviour and the Scriptures* (Wilmington: Presbyterian and Reformed, 1969); for others see W. Kenneth Cauthen, *The Impact of American Religious Liberalism* (New York; University Press of America, 1983).

[21]Letty M. Russell, *Human Liberation in a Feminist Perspective—a Theology* (Philadelphia: Westminster, 1974) is commonly found on seminary reading lists. A helpful guide produced by a Baptist is L. Faye Ignatius, *Women and Men in Church and Society* (Valley Forge: National Ministries, 1984).

tion.[22] The early church and the episcopal and connectional bodies dealt with identity-related issues by councils from at least the third century, and seventeenth century Baptists made the approach work for them.

In order to succeed, a conciliar approach first presupposes some type of group consensus, ideally a theological consensus. Where a theologically pluralistic family exists, however, other factors must replace theology, such as mission or common heritage. In the case of a predominantly white, English heritage which seeks to be multi-ethnic and multi-racial, achieving a sense of common tradition can be difficult. To offset this concern, any council which seeks to articulate identity for a Baptist group will have to reflect all of the diversities and the consensus of which the total community is composed.

A second presupposition among the free churches is that a council must carry the representative authority of the entire body. In a church polity which stresses the autonomy and even independence of individual congregations, no council can assume the right to speak for churches or organizations, unless instructed to do so. In a classic essay adopted by the Philadelphia Baptist Association in 1749, Benjamin Griffiths wrote that:

> several such independent churches, where Providence gives them their situation convenient, may and ought—for their mutual strength, counsel, and other valuable advantages—by their voluntary and free consent, to enter into an agreement and confederation . . . [23]

An echo of the limit of power and authority beyond the local congregation, Francis Wayland asserted in 1856 that "we have nothing to submit to representation . . . it is impossible that a church of Christ can be in any proper and legitimate sense, represented."[24] Forewarned by their own history of autonomy, Baptist councils must be created, empowered, and accountable to the broadest possible body of churches.

Baptists do have a history—albeit uneven—of conciliar action related to their identity.[25] As mentioned previously, the first attempts to define the Baptist ethos were confessions of faith issued by "elders, deacons and brethren" of congregations and persons who individually signed their names to the

---

[22]The American Baptist Churches in the U.S.A. in 1984 authorized a "blue ribbon commission on Denominational Identity" composed of biblical scholars, theologians and historians. The Baptist Union of Ontario and Quebec has recently completed a similar process and has produced for the consideration of their churches, *This We Believe* (Hamilton: 1986).

[23]The essay is included in A. D. Gillette, editor, *Minutes of the Philadelphia Baptist Association, 1707-1807* (Philadelphia: American Baptist Publication Society, 1851): 60-63.

[24]Francis Wayland, *Notes on the Principles and Practices of Baptist Churches* (Boston: Gould & Lincoln, 1856): 181.

[25]A beginning point, limited because of its publication date is William H. Allison, *Baptist Councils in America: A Historical Study of Their Origins and the Principles of Their Development* (Chicago: Hazlett, 1906).

confessions. The process behind such confessional statements obviously involved considerable discussion and debate within associational meetings and
the revision process for the written products. Among the General Baptists,
for instance, it was noted that on occasion, the entire gathered assembly hammered out important statements:

> Many of the Messengers, Elders, and Brethren of the Baptized churches . . .
> have also thought it necessary to Publish and Declare the Judgments and
> consciences touching the Civill Power of the nation, partly to Vindicate
> themselves from some aspersions hereabout unduly and without cause cast
> upon them; And partly to rectify all men's misapprehensions of them.[26]

The records of the Philadelphia Baptist Association also bear an eloquent
witness to the conciliar approach. Regularly in the first three decades of the
eighteenth century, Association delegates discussed issues related to identity:
terms of membership, relations with other churches and ordination. In 1742
after debate on the matter, the Association voted to adopt the Second London
Confession of Faith (1677) with two additional articles on psalm singing and
the laying on of hands. Often overlooked, both of these provisions reflected
the actual practices of Philadelphia Association churches and thus a confessional statement which had a much earlier and unique social context, was
modified to fit the shape of an American community. Somewhat uncritically,
five other American associations adopted the confession, while others in the
Separate Baptist tradition in the South initially rejected this and all confessions of faith.[27]

Most American Baptists who used a confessional statement preferred the
London/Philadelphia tradition until influenced in the early nineteenth century
by local church protectionism and Arminian theology. The first major change
came among New Hampshire Baptists who desired ''a Declaration of Faith
and Practice, together with a Covenant, as may be thought agreeable and consistent with the views of this state.'' New Hampshire Baptists admitted what
others had not realized; evolving circumstances had forged a new identity
which was more moderately Calvinistic with a sharper focus on the local congregation. The resultant New Hampshire Confession of Faith, adopted in
1833, was actually the work of a committee of four persons appointed by the
State Convention to write a new statement of faith. What is not known is that

---

[26]William T. Whitley, editor, *Minutes of the General Assembly of the General Baptist
Churches in England* (London: Baptist Historical Society, 1909) 1:2.

[27]Those who accepted the confession were the Charleston (S.C.), Warrren (R.I.), Ketoc-
tan (Va.), Elkhorn (Kty.) and Holston (Tenn.) associations; opposed were the Separates in
VA. before 1783 and the Kehukee in N.C.

the finished product was never presented to the Convention body for adoption and was not mentioned in the Convention proceedings after 1833.[28]

The New Hampshire Confession enjoyed a new lease on life when J. Newton Brown, one of the original committee members in the New Hampshire State Convention, added two articles ("On Repentance and Faith" and "On Sanctification") and reissued the confession through the American Baptist Publication Society. Brown was then the book editor of the Society and used his position to create a new—and I would argue artificial—authority for a confession that was rooted in a specific theological and social context. In the later nineteenth century, the Brown version was added to several Baptist polity manuals and it achieved a renewed popularity among the Landmark churches, who were especially fond of its advocacy of local congregations.[29]

Even more amazing was the popularity of the New Hampshire Confession among Fundamentalists in the 1920s and 1940s in the Northern Convention and in the 1920s among Southern Baptists. In the Northern churches, Fundamentalist leaders called for a rigid and specific adherence to a set of "Articles of Faith" which prompted moderates to turn to the New Hampshire Confession. Ultimately, the Northern Baptist Convention in 1922 turned aside all confessional statements and affirmed its support of the New Testament alone as the authority for faith and practice. A splinter group of the N.B.C., called the General Association of Regular Baptists, adopted in 1932 the New Hampshire Confession as its doctrinal standard.[30]

Acting under the influence of both the Landmarkers and Fundamentalists, Southern Baptists in 1925 also adopted a modified version of the New Hampshire document. To the original articles were added statements on issues such as peace and war, social service, and education, and the original articles on law and government and the civil government were deleted. The final statement, which the Convention messengers approved and which was printed in the official minutes, was the work of a distinguished committee composed of men such as E. Y. Mullins, L. R. Scarborough and W. J. McGlothlin, the latter an expert on the history of Baptist confessions of faith.

---

[28]"Records of the New Hampshire Baptist State Convention," 1830-1835 in Archives, American Baptist Historical Society. One can speculate that the influence of Francis Wayland which was anti-confessional, or a lack of enthusiasm among the churches, led to its neglect as an official confession in New Hampshire.

[29]J. Newton Brown, *The Baptist Church Manual* (Philadelphia: American Baptist Publication Society, 1853); James Pendleton, *Church Manual, Designed for the Use of Baptist Churches* (Philadelphia, A.B.P.S., 1867); Edward T. Hiscox, *The Baptist Church Directory* (New York; Sheldon, 1859).

[30]The Saga of the G.A.R.B.C. is found in Joseph M. Stowell, *Background and History of the General Association of Regular Baptists* (Chicago: Gospel Tracts Unlimited, 1949) 71-80. This useful book also includes the doctrinal statement, constitution, and bylaws.

In 1963 Herschel Hobbs chaired a committee to again revise what had come to be known as the "Baptist Faith and Message" and the Southern Baptists continued in the tradition of the New Hampshire Baptist Confession of faith.

The significant negative impact of the confessionalism among Baptists is illustrated in the Fundamentalist wing of the Northern Baptist Convention. In 1921 Frank M. Goodchild, an Iowa Baptist pastor, presented a simple confessional statement to the Northern Baptist Convention which was predictably defeated. The Goodchild Confession lay fallow until a second schism opened in the Northern Convention in the 1940s over the inclusive policy of the Foreign Mission Society. When the resultant Conservative Baptist Foreign Mission Society (later the Conservative Baptist Association) was organized in 1943, the Goodchild Confession became its doctrinal statement with the following restriction in the preamble: "only those persons who, without reservation, fully and freely subscribe to the following doctrinal statement are eligible to vote." A second provision limited officers, employees, and missionaries to those who likewise would sign the statement.[31] Contrary to the three hundred year old confessional tradition of mainstream Baptists, a statement of identity had become a tool of discipline and the confession of faith, voluntarily expressive of a group, became the work of one individual who was not even a part of the group which adopted the statement. Moreover, it was significant that the terminology "doctrinal statement" replaced "confession of faith" and a new religious test was inaugurated. The only differences between a doctrinal statement and a creed among such Baptists was that subscribers did not recite the doctrinal statement in worship and the statements lacked the linguistic grandeur of the old creeds. Practically, the doctrinal statements were used in the same manner as the creeds were in the ancient church.

Witnessing this trend as a violation of the historic Baptist principle of religious liberty, both the American and Southern Conventions have declined to adopt strict confessional statements. The A.B.C. has continued to affirm its confidence in the New Testament and the S.B.C. has carefully defined its most recent "Baptist Faith and Message" statement as guiding principles which are not binding or to be used as a test of faith.[32] Because a sense of identity is clearer among the non-aligned groups of Baptists which all have

---

[31]Materials in Frank M. Goodchild are in the Records of the Ministers and Missionaries Benefit Board, Archives, American Baptist Historical Society; his confession is printed in *The Chronicle* 7 (April 1944): 57-58.

[32]No more recent statement has been made than the position taken at Grand Rapids in 1946. See *Yearbook of the Northern Baptist Convention* (1946) 96-97; for Southern Baptists, consult *Annual of the Southern Baptist Convention* (1963) 63, 269-81 for the report of the Committee on "Baptist Faith and Message."

doctrinal statements, persons within both American and Southern Baptist ranks combine to press for at least a confessional statement. Again, it is evident that forces external to both the major conventions are helping to create a negative identity and an identity crisis for both the A.B.C. and S.B.C., not unlike what happened to seventeenth century English and American Baptists.[33] One alternative which mainstream Baptists must consider is that of creating representative councils to assent to positive and acceptable statements of identity.

FINALLY, AN OBSERVATION AND A PROPOSAL

For those who stand outside the ideological and practical squabbling of the people called Baptist and wonder what a Baptist is, there is an answer. What all Baptists have in common is their practice of believer's baptism and the theology which accompanies it. The earliest congregations referred to themselves as "churches of Christ," "baptized Congregations," or "organized according to the primitive pattern" only to be ridiculed and publicly denounced as "Anabaptists." Beyond the desire to defame the baptizers by associating them with the most reactionary Christians of the era, adversaries made the clear connection of believers' baptism. Daniel Featley, an Anglican controversialist and ardent opponent of the Baptists, said of the "Dippers": "They preach and print and practice their impieties openly . . . they flock in great multitudes to their Jordans . . . the presses sweat and groan under the load of their blasphemies."[34] And, to fulfill the expectations of their adversaries, Baptists spent a good deal of time in their first century disputing the baptism of infants on the testimony of scripture.

At the turn of the eighteenth century, Baptists themselves recognized their uniqueness and began referring to themselves as "churches of the baptized way" or in the Philadelphia tradition, "churches holding believer's baptism." This last designation was indeed insightful for it allowed Baptists to be liberated from the charge of sacramentarianism and what emerged was a broader sense of identity that was adequately symbolized in baptism. Baptists ever since, and to their credit, have hammered away at that mark of identity which has provided a unique contribution to Christian history.

In the Baptist heritage, baptism is an immediate statement about the gospel and the church. In contrast to other Christian traditions, in which baptism

---

[33]The forces now include Pat Robertson, a television evangelist and former Southern Baptist and Jerry Falwell who, while he is pastor of an independent Baptist church in Lynchburg, VA, in 1984 was voted by a national poll to be the most influential person in Southern Baptist life.

[34]Daniel Featley, *The Dippers Dipt or The Anabaptists Ducked and Plunged over Head and Eares at a Disputation in Southwark* (London: n.p., 1645) 6.

is focused upon the candidate or sponsors, or the grace-mediating role of the
Church, for Baptists, baptism is a public identification with the gospel. The
earliest statements by Baptists indicate that baptism was to them much more
than a symbol. Rather, it was a bold, public profession of a relationship with
Jesus Christ: his death, burial and resurrection. The act further signified fellowship with Christ, remission of sins and an intent ''to walk in newness of
life.''[35]

From 1640 the mode of baptism was also significant to Baptists. Differing from Anabaptists, early Baptists found scriptural justification for immersion and infused the mode with a rich meaning. No other technique could
adequately express the whole gospel as believers' baptism by immersion did.
Few sermons could present as eloquently as a baptism, how Baptists understood the gospel.

In their historic statements about the nature of the Church, Baptists have
frequently used the terminology ''baptized believers.'' This has led critics to
assume that Baptists thus created a new legalistic restriction on their definition of the Church which clearly set it apart from other Christian fellowships.
Actually, early Baptists used the term ''baptized'' in an adjectival sense, that
is to indicate that through their own baptisms as believers, congregational
members each appropriated the richness of their theology of baptism in their
own religious experiences and thus established a common bond in the community of the congregation.[36] Naturally, only ''those who do actually profess
repentance towards God, faith in, and obedience to our Lord Jesus,'' should
be baptized and therefore enjoy the benefits of the Church.

More than any other characteristic of the Baptist tradition, then, believers' baptism by immersion was the functional essence of historic Baptist
identity. For those who claimed to reconstitute primitive Christianity, the ordinance spoke literally from the New Testament of the salient issues in the
gospel, and of a voluntary personal relationship with Jesus Christ. Criticized
heavily, but convinced of its relevance, virtually all Baptists have been united
on the issue of baptism. Little wonder that America's first Baptist historian,
the eminent Morgan Edwards of Philadelphia, asserted that ''Practising believer's baptism is our denominating article.''[37]

---

[35]The Phrase was first used in John Smyth's covenant, established at Gainsborough about
1606. The story is told in Roger Hayden, ''To Walk in All His Ways'' *Christian History* 4:2
(Spring, 1985).

[36]Art. 13, ''A Short Confession by John Smyth''; Art. xxxiii, ''First London Confession''; art. xii, ''The Standard Confession''; art. xxix, ''Second London Confession''; art.
xxviii, ''The Orthodox Creed''; art. xiii, ''New Hampshire Confession of Faith''; art. xiii,
''Articles of Faith,'' Baptist Bible Union of America. In each case, the term ''baptized believer'' is operant.

[37]Morgan Edwards, *Materials Toward A History of the Baptists in Pennsylvania* (Philadelphia: Cruikshank, 1770) 1.

If all Baptists share a common denominator in our doctrine of baptism, we must also painfully admit that we are, beyond that affirmation, hopelessly fragmented. Theological, political, and social realities are such that Baptists have spread in many directions and categories. While we have pressed our basic principle successfully, we have blunted our concern for scriptural Christianity by disagreeing on virtually every detail mentioned in the Bible. The solution to this fragmentation has been the natural clustering of churches into associations or communions which can agree on enough principles to co-operate in fellowship and service.[38]

That being the case, it naturally follows that Baptists *ought* (to use Benjamin Griffith's word) to enter into agreements and confederations. Moreover, every such confederation has the right and responsibility to define its own identity. As a people with a confessional history, Baptists know that while they may not have a holistically unique theology, they can agree on operating theological principles. While no two lists of Baptist principles are exactly alike, churches with a similar heritage and mission outlook can agree on matters of priority and concern. Mere pluralism or diversity, as American Baptist General Secretary, Robert Campbell has observed, "is a lousy identity."[39] Given the broadest possible participation in the creation of such agreements and the voluntary ratification of ideas and principles, an appropriate confession results, which is as much a movement of God's Spirit in consensus as perspicuity of the leadership. Confessional statements of this kind which are constantly scrutinized and revised where necessary, enable a positive bonding process which needs no negative sanctions or discipline. As the historical record well illustrates, Baptist life and mission have thrived each time a consensus has been reached within a communion and a clearer sense of identity has emerged. Individual confessions can create a polyglot beauty in the midst of fragmentation as Baptist Christians work together in the visible Kingdom. To put it theologically, as each congregation is distinct in its character, so each voluntarily derived component of associational life is also distinct. An identity for the Baptist denomination is thus the sum of all its parts, which comes as no surprise to any student of the Free Church tradition.

Baptist history is replete with self-doubt and identity crises. Even in moments of great exultation, such as the sesquicentennial in 1964 of the found-

---

[38]There are, at present, in excess of twenty-five distinct Baptist groups in the United States. Some are local/regional clusters, some theologically separate, others racially distinct. Identity within these groups is established primarily in one of two ways: (a) a statement of historical relationships (National Baptists); (b) a confessional statement (General Association of Regular Baptists).

[39]"General Secretary's Report to the General Board," December 1983 in Records of the ABC General Board, Archives, American Baptist Historical Society.

ing of organized missionary work in the United States, an insightful Baptist
historian named Robert G. Torbet wrote:

> In our day when the trend in religion is toward unity, Baptists, like other
> denominations, need to define themselves in terms of who they are, what
> their purposes are, and what their role is within the total Christian fellow-
> ship. Some Baptists are presently acknowledging this need; others are not.
> Certainly, this kind of a self-examination is not easy; it has its own built-in
> dangers. For example, there is a hazard of confusing self-identity with self-
> aggrandizement and seeking to justify existence as a denomination by false
> claims of superiority. There is also a danger of overemphasizing the group's
> distinctiveness in order to justify its independent existence or to reinforce a
> claim that it is in some sense exclusively "the true church."[40]

Ironically, his words could have been written yesterday.

---

[40]Robert G. Torbet and Samuel S. Hill, *Baptists North and South* (Valley Forge: Judson, 1964) 14.

THE ESSENCE
OF THE BAPTISTS:
A REEXAMINATION

ERIC H. OHLMANN
NORTHERN BAPTIST THEOLOGICAL SEMINARY
LOMBARD IL 60148

Computer hacks remind us of the treasures one can access by knowing the code. Deciphering the entry code to a piece of computer software makes all the difference between gaining access to all that it offers or not even stealing a glimpse at its secrets. While not that decisive, decoding the essence of a movement produces similar benefits. It can unlock and reveal the true inner dynamics of a movement and serve as a secret map to its intellectual terrain. Yet Baptists have not particularly focused on the task of determining their own inner reality, with the result that they are uncertain about their true identity.

During much of their history, Baptists were fairly confident about their identity. They were especially sure about their distinctive beliefs and practices, because they were regularly called upon to defend those deviations from "mainline" denominations. With this self-perception usually came a strong sense of purpose, denominational vitality and the determination to pursue the Baptist mission against all odds.

Today, Baptists, and especially American Baptists, are much less sure of their identity. We are vague about characteristic Baptist thinking in the past, about distinctive Baptist institutional structures and polity, about distinguishing Baptist ideals and loyalties. We are even less sure of what constitutes an appropriate Baptist identity today. Nor is it merely a case of poorly informed laypersons. The professional church leaders share this perplexity. It is as though an epidemic of denominational amnesia has set in.

This uncertainty creates serious problems. Not knowing what rightfully belongs to our heritage, we are inadvertently and wrecklessly discarding some priceless heirlooms. Furthermore, as with amnesia patients, our confusion makes for disorientation, aimlessness and ineffectivensss. It makes for difficulty in living with ourselves and for even greater difficulty in relating to others. In the case of an entire denomination, the severity multiplies, robbing that body of its mission, its very reason for being. For without a sense of identity and purpose a movement does not know why or which way to move. Clearly, the stakes are high.

Numerous books and articles have been penned over the years in an effort to rectify this problem. Some scanned the entire gamut of so-called Baptist distinctives, while others probed only one or more leading characteristic. Most writers did not attempt any prioritizing of Baptist traits (although some of them may have implied a ranking by the order in which they treated the subjects). But a few delineated a list of characteristic Baptist emphases and also sought to locate the central tenet of Baptist thought or foundation for the superstructure.

This article aims only at the latter. Its purpose is not to paint another composite portrait of Baptists but rather to reopen the question, What is the essence of Baptists? What is their primary characteristic, the decisive organizing principle of their thought. In less abstract terms, What have they valued above all else? What was the principal motivation for their actions? The conclusion is significantly different from the prevailing view today.

The approach here is both historical and theological, though primarily theological. Thorough historical documentation of the thesis would be an extensive undertaking and would far exceed the intended scope of this article. Therefore, the objective will be to identify the fundamental nature of Baptist life and thought and the interrelationships of its various parts, primarily by tracing some of the theology and logic involved.

Although Baptists have changed and diversified significantly over the centuries, it is assumed that the Baptist movement had an identifiable essence from the start and has retained it intact.[1] The primary historical focus, therefore, will be on the formative years of Baptists in England, and only secondary attention will be afforded subsequent changes and developments. Although Baptists have not always been given to profound theological reflection, it is also assumed that their movement has an internal logic and that one can logically excavate the theological premises of the movement, ascertain the de-

---

[1]Despite momentous developments and changes among Baptists, presumably no one would argue that the movement has undergone an essential mutation, in the sense that it is no longer its original self and has become an essentially different movement.

rivation of its other characteristics from that basis and determine their logical interrelations.[2]

A study of this nature, admittedly, has liabilities as well as benefits. It may be viewed as an attempt to simplify or reduce a complex movement to one central characteristic. Baptists have been too diverse and complex to be reduced in that manner, nor is that the intent here. It is rather to understand better the complexity of the movement by an analysis which involves locating its basis and unraveling its organizing principle. Besides, the benefits more than warrant the risk. Knowing the essence of a movement can serve as the entry code to that movement. It can provide a new and insightful angle of vision; provide a new formative principle by which to relate and understand its parts; identify the underlying motivation, greatly illuminating its system of thought, institutional structures and polity and its general mode of behavior. The aspirations for this investigation are to contribute to those ends.

What then is the essence of Baptists? What is their inner nature? What is that foundation on which the superstructure rests or the hub from which the particulars radiate? What is the value which Baptists have cherished more than others or which has been the underlying motivation for the Baptist mission?

CONSISTENT ADHERENCE TO SCRIPTURE

Complete dependence upon Scripture and consistent obedience to it has been proposed by some as the primary characteristic of Baptists and the principal foundation of their beliefs and practices.[3] As contrasted to Christian groups who intentionally draw upon sources such as tradition, reason and experience, in addition to the Bible, for guidance in religious matters, it is contended that Baptists have regularly and emphatically held to Scripture alone as their sole authority for faith and practice, to the point of denying even confessions of faith any creedal status and that this solitary adherence to Scripture best accounts for their peculiar characteristics. The Modernist-Fundamentalist controversy consolidated support of this interpretation among those who fear that some present-day Baptists take Scripture too lightly.

It has also been contended that the best explanation for the differences between Baptists and the Magisterial Reformation is the former's more con-

---

[2]This process is often difficult when a movement has a single founder. The difficulty increases proportionately with the number of movers and shapers, and in the case of the Baptists they were myriad. Nevertheless, the essence of Baptists is subject to logical analysis.

[3]E.g., F. Wayland, *The Principles and Practices of Baptist Churches* (London: J. Heaton & Son, 1861) 30, 63; Carl F. H. Henry, "Twenty Years a Baptist," *Foundations* 1 (January 1958): 47; and L. Russ Bush and Tom J. Nettles, *Baptists and the Bible* (Chicago: Moody Press, 1980) 18.

sistent and courageous adherence to the Bible. Offered as evidence of this
claim is the unwavering Baptist adherence to believers' baptism, religious
liberty and the separation of church and state, despite the fact that they were
unpopular and revolutionary ideas.[4]

The advent of religious liberty and voluntarism in America, resulting in
an open market for church members, solicited more explicit claims of Baptist
superiority over other denominations in their loyalty to Scripture in an effort
to compete. In fact, these circumstances contributed to probably the most
striking expression of this position in the successionist theory of Baptist origins
and especially the Landmarkist use of it. For the thrust of the Landmarkist
case was that Baptists are the present-day link in a chain of Christian groups
who have retained the marks of the New Testament church throughout the
centuries and therefore best reflect the biblical position.

While it is true that Baptists have diligently sought to adhere to the Bible,
this theory is not without its problems. Baptists have been profoundly influenced and shaped by the Reformed tradition, by Puritanism in particular and
by their own religious experiences. Nor have they been immune from non-
religious influences as some seem to claim. Like all religious movements,
they have been constantly and significantly impacted by prevailing systems
of thought and many other non-religious factors. And, naturally their interpretation of Scripture has been colored by all of these influences. To claim
otherwise would be untrue and more detrimental than beneficial; if sources
of religious authority do not include tradition, reason and experience, they
are deficient.

Secondly, since all Christians seek to be faithful to the scriptures, it is
somewhat arrogant for any one denomination to claim that it has succeeded
better than the rest. Furthermore, one can not substantiate such a claim, since
much of the Bible lends itself to different interpretations. Who, for instance,
has the right interpretation of the New Testament pattern for church governance? One may—indeed must—adopt certain positions, adhere to them in
faith and be prepared to advocate them, but one can not prove one's own interpretations to be superior.

Interestingly, early Baptists did not consider themselves distinctive in their
use of Scripture; their articles of faith regarding the Bible basically repeated
the prevailing views among Puritans. How could the Baptist use of Scripture
then have distinguished them from the Puritans?

Lastly, this theory focuses more on means than on ends; it comes closer
to an explanation of *how* Baptists may have arrived at their beliefs and cus-
toms than an account of *what* constitutes their intrinsic being. Surely, what a

---

[4]Wayland, *Principles* XXI, 93-96.

religious body believes is more foundational to its identity than how it arrived at its belief system. And most Baptists would not claim the Bible itself as the object of their faith.

RELIGIOUS LIBERTY

Solicitude for religious liberty has also been put forward as the heartbeat of Baptists. They lived as disadvantaged and persecuted sectarians in England for centuries, in most of the American colonies and still find themselves in that situation in many other countries. Their circumstances, therefore, have constantly cried out for religious liberty, the freedom to follow their consciences in religious matters without any outside interference.

Furthermore, because this idea was very revolutionary during the first centuries of Baptist life, severely threatened the existing power structures and was vehemently resisted, Baptists were highly energized by the notion, wrote more on the subject than on any other[5] and fought more persistently to achieve it. Fervent advocacy of this principle also helps to account for differences between themselves and the Puritans, with whom they agreed at most other points.

Theologically, Baptists have understood religious liberty as an integral part of Christianity, which by its very nature requires voluntary, intentional responses to God's grace. In time they also came to view religious liberty as part of the image of God in mankind and therefore an inherent and inalienable right. Thus, it is not surprising that E. Y. Mullins "intuited" and E. Glenn Hinson has asserted that "the essence of our tradition lies in the conviction that faith must be free, a voluntary response to God."[6]

From Baptist life and thought it is clear that a commitment to religious liberty lies close to the heart of Baptists. It has been vigorously defended, tenaciously adhered to and strenuously advocated. Nothing else has generated as much forceful attack by Baptists upon their opponents or been undertaken at a greater cost to life and property. It also is a significant point of demarcation between Baptists and the Puritans. Yet, does it constitute the soul of the Baptists? Although indispensable to Christianity, religious liberty is essentially the freedom to express one's faith. And are Baptists prepared to

---

[5]See, e.g., H. Leon McBeth, *English Baptist Literature on Religious Liberty to 1689* (New York: Arno Press, 1980).

[6]James Leo Garrett, E. Glenn Hinson, and James E. Tull, *Are Southern Baptists "Evangelicals"?* (Macon, Ga.: Mercer University Press, 1983), p. 140. See also John Quincy Adams, *Baptists, The Only Thorough Reformers*. Revised and Enlarged ed. (New York: U. D. Wood, Publishers, 1876) 96-97; James E. Wood, ed., *Baptists and the American Experience* (Valley Forge: Judson Press, 1976) 20.

grant that the freedom to express their faith has been more important than the religious faith which they have expressed? Religious liberty is not of much value unless those who enjoy its benefits have meaningful beliefs to profess and practice. It was an indispensable means, but primarily a means to a greater end. Or, recognizing that religious liberty was also a part of the Baptists' system of beliefs, one may more accurately ask, Has the right to live out their faith been more important than any other element of their thought? It is rather telling that even the major Baptists advocates of religious liberty did not think so.

SOUL COMPETENCY

Similarly, some have identified a particular component of religious liberty as the central tenet of Baptists. Most prominent among these is the contention that Baptists have held most firmly to the right and ability of the individual to approach God directly, without any human intermediary. In Baptist parlance this concept is usually referred to as soul liberty or soul competency. Based on a historical and philosophical analysis of Baptists, E. Y. Mullins concluded in 1908 that the soul's competency in religion is the one comprehensive truth from which all other Baptist traits logically follow.[7] Others have perpetuated that interpretation since.[8]

The limitations of this view are basically the same as those of the broader religious liberty position. Soul liberty has been a valuable weapon against sacerdotalism and a propitious ideological foundation for the priesthood of all believers. It certainly has penetrated deeply into the Baptist spirit, especially in America, where it has been intensified by Rationalism's insistence on religion as a personal matter between the individual and God, by revivalism's emphasis on a personal decision of faith and by the American enchantment with civil and religious liberty. But is even the right and ability to approach God directly more basic than one's relationship to God itself. Surely the two cannot be compared. A meaningful relationship to God can be greatly hampered by outside restrictions. But soul liberty is only the right and ability to relate to God directly, and isn't that relationship itself the prior and basic issue?

---

[7]E. Y. Mullins, *The Axioms of Religion: A New Interpretation of the Baptist Faith* (Philadelphia: American Baptist Publication Society, 1908) 53-57.

[8]E.g., William Roy McNutt, *Polity and Practice in Baptist Churches* (Philadelphia: The Judson Press, 1935), 21-25; H. W. Robinson, *The Life and Faith of the Baptists* (London: The Kingsgate Press, 1946) 19, 24.

AUTONOMY OF THE LOCAL CHURCH—SEPARATION OF CHURCH AND STATE

Other interpreters of the Baptists have focused on the autonomy of the local congregation[9] or the separation of church and state, two further expressions of religious liberty. Landmarkist Baptists, in particular, have constantly punctuated the right of each local congregation to determine its own beliefs, polity and leadership as one of the major marks of the New Testament churches and subsequently of Baptists.

The Baptist emphasis on and strenuous struggle for religious liberty has led others to conclude that the separation of church and state has been the major agenda. Opposition to any state control over matters of religion set Baptists and the Separatists apart from the rest of the Puritans, and to this day Baptists cooperate more with each other on this issue than on any other.[10] Logically and practically, the separation of church and state is a necessary social corollary of religious liberty; true religious freedom can only exist when the state is not in a position to dictate matters of religion. Therefore, this preoccupation of the Baptists follows from their commitment to religious liberty. It is also the area in which Baptists have made a major contribution to the rest of the world.

These two convictions are the ground rules by which local Baptist congregations relate to their sister churches and by which Baptists relate to the larger political entities of which they are a part. They are crucial rights and have played a major role in Baptist resistance to outside authorities. Yet, these principles are essentially by-products of the broader concept of religious liberty and also beg the question of importance and priority. Are they not important primarily because they allow certain freedoms and practices? But is the freedom greater than what it allows? Is the freedom of a local congregation to determine its own destiny, for example, more important than the mission it seeks to fulfill? Or is the freedom from state restrictions more important than the faith and practice which might be restricted?

EVANGELISM AND MISSIONS

Taking their clues from activities in which Baptists have invested most energy and at which they have done best, some have submitted that Baptists have been most characterized by involvement in evangelism and missions.[11]

---

[9]J. R. Graves, *Old Landmarkism: What is It?* 2nd ed. (Memphis: Baptist Book House, 1881) 35-52; J. M. Pendleton, *Distinctive Principles of Baptists* (Philadelphia: American Baptist Publication Society, 1882) 169-224.

[10]The reference here is to the Baptist Joint Committee on Public Affairs which is a cooperative Baptist body devoted largely to the protection of the separation of church and state.

While not alleging that evangelism is the essence of Baptists, E. Glenn Hinson has asserted that "nothing is more evident than that Southern Baptists are committed to evangelism as the overriding concern."[12]

Much can be said for this perspective. Although founded nearly a century after the Reformation and discriminated against most of the time since then, Baptists have become the largest Protestant denomination in the United States and one of the largest in the world. That record speaks volumes. Secondly, all Baptist denominational structures were organized primarily for mission purposes. Evangelism and missions were also products of the central Baptist tenet advanced in this article.

But a major problem with this thesis is that Baptists have not always been evangelistic or mission-minded. Few would contend that the Particular Baptists, who most shaped Baptist life and thought over the years, were especially noteworthy for their evangelistic efforts or for their involvement in missions during the first one-and-a-half centuries of their life. Even after that they only gradually became more evangelistic—in England through the influence of the Wesleyan revivals and in America through the influence of the Great Awakening, the Separate Baptists, particularly the Second Great Awakening, the need to compete in a voluntary context and reaction to the Social Gospel.

Further, this attempt to understand Baptists is not complete without asking why Baptists have been so solicitous of evangelism and missions. Such vigilance must have had some basis. Would they have expended so much effort at these tasks if they did not have some prior or underlying reason, some compelling motivation to do so? If there were no such reason, then why invite persons to believe the gospel and to make a commitment to Christ and why engage in other facets of missions?

IMMERSION

Believing that the essence of Baptists is found in their most distinctive features, some have singled out the practice of baptism by immersion. Initially, such judgments were usually made by outside observers, especially mockers of the Baptist practice. In subsequent years, however, some Baptists came to concur with this assessment, and in the nineteenth century, the Landmarkists catapulted it to prominence. By maintaining that only baptism by

---

[11]Albert McClellan, "Bold Mission Thrust of Baptists, Past and Present," *Baptist History and Heritage* 14 (January 1979): 3.

[12]E. Glenn Hinson, "Southern Baptists: A Concern for Experiential Conversion," in *Where the Spirit Leads: American Denominations Today*, ed. Martin E. Marty (Atlanta: John Knox Press, 1980) 147.

immersion was valid,[13] they made the mode of baptism *the* issue of contention between Baptists and most other denominations, even denying the Lord's Supper to those not baptized by this mode. Others have kept the issue alive to this day,[14] especially in countries where immersionists are a small minority.

Baptism by immersion is important to Baptists because of what it symbolizes, and they still quickly rally to its defense. But most Baptists have generally regarded the issue of who should be baptized as more important than how it is done. More importantly, the ordinance itself, in whatever mode, is understood as an outward expression of a deeper, inner reality. Therefore, one needs to look further for the essence of Baptists.

BELIEVERS' BAPTISM

Pressing this issue one step further, many have identified believers' baptism as the quintessent Baptist characteristic. It was the baptism of conscious believers which primarily differentiated Baptists from the Puritans, and, throughout much of their history, it has been this principle which has set Baptists apart from most other denominations. For this reason, few other traits of the Baptist family have required as much defense and have been written about as extensively.

Believers' baptism is clearly an integral part of being Baptist. It is a major denominational distinctive and has been expounded upon ad nauseam. Yet, it is not self-explanatory and leaves one wondering why it has been so important to Baptists. All of them have emphatically insisted that it is not necessary for salvation, and many have even conceded that it is not necessary as a prerequisite for church membership. Does not its importance rest on the prior and pervasive stress that Baptists have placed on personal, intentional faith and active commitment of one's life to Christ. Even for someone as early as John Smyth, believers' baptism was considered to be for persons already in covenant relationship with God, with priority on the covenantal relationship.[15] Believers' baptism also gains some of its impact as derivative of a believers' church; for most Baptists it is one step in the admissions process to such a church.

---

[13]J. M. Pendleton, *An Old Landmark Re-set* (Nashville: South Western Publishing House, 1857) 5-9; J. M. Pendleton, *Three Reasons Why I am a Baptist* (Cincinnati: Moore, Anderson & Company, 1853) 82-137.

[14]Edward T. Hiscox, *The New Directory for Baptist Churches* (Philadelphia: The Judson Press, 1894) 123. The issue has also resurfaced in numerous editorials and articles on open membership, appearing in Baptist periodicals, especially since about 1930.

[15]B. R. White, *The English Separatist Tradition: From the Marian Martyrs to the Pilgrim Fathers* (London: Oxford University Press, 1971) 135.

BELIEVERS' CHURCH

The predominant view today contends that the essence of Baptists, or at least their primary distinctiveness, is found in their concept of the church. As contrasted to inclusive state churches, Baptists have maintained that visible, local congregations should be constituted only of those who have experienced God's grace, have been baptized and have voluntarily covenanted to participate in the mission of the Church. More than any other denomination they have deplored the spiritual state of inclusive churches and consistently advocated believers' churches as a means of renewal. Behind their distinctive practice of believers' baptism, therefore, is the prior conviction that churches should be composed of regenerate believers only. That belief was reinforced by the revivalist emphasis on conversion as a prerequisite to church membership. And in 1923 William T. Whitley, a prominent Baptist historian, joined others in asserting that "the distinctive feature about Baptists is their doctrine of the Church."[16] Owing to ecumenical discussions on the nature of the Church and other factors, that perspective has been frequently reaffirmed since.[17] Surprisingly, it has gone largely unchallenged.

This diagnosis of the Baptists has a solid historical and theological basis. The founding fathers of the Baptists were most agreed in their dissatisfaction with the Church of England and in their proposal of believers' churches as the best solution to the problem. Since then, this idea has been recognized as a vitally important Baptist "distinctive"; it has been the subject of endless expositions by Baptists; and most of the other characteristic Baptist emphases are ecclesiastical issues which in one way or another stem from the idea of believers' churches.

Is, however, even this theory fully convincing? The inquiring mind still wants to know why it has been so important to constitute congregations of believers only. Does its importance lie in the principle itself or does it derive from an even deeper and prior conviction about the importance of being believers?[18] Did Baptists emerge primarily in reaction to inclusive membership

---

[16]*A History of British Baptists* (Philadelphia: J. B. Lippincott, 1923) 4.

[17]Henry Cook, *What Baptists Stand For*, 4th ed. (London: The Carey Kingsgate Press, 1961) 17, 32; Norman H. Maring and Winthrop S. Hudson, *A Baptist Manual of Polity and Practice* (Chicago: The Judson Press, 1963) 15, 17. The following trilogy has also focused unprecedented attention on Baptist ecclesiology: Duke W. McCall, comp. and ed., *What is the Church?* (Nashville: Broadman Press, 1958); Winthrop S. Hudson, ed., *Baptist Concepts of the Church* (Chicago: The Judson Press, 1959); A. Gilmore, ed., *The Pattern of the Church: A Baptist View* (London: Lutterworth Press, 1963).

[18]See, for example, White, *Separatist Tradition* 122-29.

in state churches or in reaction to the effect of state churches upon the moral and spiritual lives of its members? To ask the question another way, Has the basic issue for Baptists been ecclesiological or soteriological? It would be somewhat ironic if a sectarian movement which emerged out of reaction to a churchly tradition and which constantly resisted that tradition from the depth of its instincts would center its own life around an ecclesiological issue, even though it were the vital issue of criteria for church membership. Nor is it convincing that the material principle of the church lay closest to their hearts, gave rise to their movement, and has been the primary motivating force in their lives. There must be another key to understanding the Baptists, a better and more inclusive explanation for their daring and aggressive enterprises.

QUALITY CHRISTIAN LIVING

Sixteenth century Puritanism provides valuable clues. After all, Baptists emerged out of Puritanism: most early Baptists, including their leaders, had been Puritans before becoming Baptists.[19] Nor did they discard their Puritan ideals and aspiration upon identifying with the Baptists. According to their most widely used confessions of faith[20] and subsequent claims throughout their history, commonalities with the Puritans, even after decades and centuries of separate existence, still far exceeded differences between them. Rather than abandon their Puritan roots, Baptists usually intensified those characteristics, resulting in them being designated the left-wing of the Puritan movement. What then did Baptists adopt from their Puritan roots and influences which speak to their deepest instincts and goals?

The essence of Puritanism itself has been subject to numerous interpretations. All of them agree that the Puritans were dissatisfied with the Church of England and sought to renew it but then diverge beyond that point, because different groups within Puritanism adopted different means of accomplishing this common goal. Yet, most interpreters have found the essence of Puritanism in some facet of their soteriology: Herbert Wallace Schneider and Perry Miller in covenant theology (especially as it applied to soteriology); William Haller in intense introspection into the working of the law of predestination within their own souls; M. M. Knappen in the moral consciousness of the saints; Geoffrey F. Nuttall in the search for a purer way of life; Owen C. Watkins in conversion and the Christian life; Sacvan Bercovitch in their view of man, to which they correlated their doctrine of salvation; and R. T. Kendall

---

[19]Winthrop S. Hudson, ''Baptists Were Not Anabaptists,'' *The Chronicle* 16 (October 1953): 173.

[20]Second London Confession and The Orthodox Creed.

in knowledge of saving faith.[21] More specifically, Alan Simpson has proposed:

> The essence of Puritanism . . . is an experience of conversion which separates the Puritan from the mass of mankind and endows him with the privileges and the duties of the elect. The root of the matter is always a new birth, which brings with it a conviction of salvation and a dedication to warfare against sin.

The whole object of the Puritans' existence, he went on to say, was to trace this experience in themselves and to produce it in others.[22] Because of our total depravity and incapacity for any spiritual good, we need to be reborn,[23] and the ideal of at least the first generation was intense piety.[24] Not only that but "Puritanism never offered itself as anything but a doctrine of salvation."[25]

As a derivative of this central conviction, Separatist Puritans—and in time also the rest—embraced the notion of limiting church membership to visible saints. Believing that the new birth visibly separates the saints from the polluted mass of mankind, they dared to close the gap between the visible and the invisible church. They did not claim infallibility in determining who was or was not regenerate, but they felt obligated at least to aim at approximating the invisible church in the local congregation.[26]

It is instructive to view these developments through a wide-angle lens which encompasses the entire Reformation. In medieval Roman Catholicism salvation could be acquired only through the Church; it was heavily dependent upon the sacraments, administered by priests who had been duly authorized by the Church. Both the source and sustaining power for the Christian life were supernatural and under the authority of someone else. In contrast, "Luther's formulation," alleges Sacvan Bercovitch,

---

[21]Wallace Herbert Schneider, *The Puritan Mind* (New York: Henry Holt and Company, 1930); Perry Miller, *The New England Mind: The Seventeen Century* (New York: The Macmillan Company, 1939); William Haller, *The Rise of Puritanism* (New York: Columbia University Press, 1957); M. M. Knappen, *Tudor Puritanism: A Chapter in the History of Idealism* (Chicago: University of Chicago Press, 1939); Geoffrey F. Nuttall, *The Puritan Spirit* (London: Epworth Press, 1967); Owen C. Watkins, *The Puritan Experience: Studies in Spiritual Autobiographies* (New York: Schocken Books, 1972); Sacvan Bercovitch, *The Puritan Origins of the American Self* (New Haven: Yale University Press, 1975); R. T. Kendall, *Calvin and English Calvinism to 1649* (Oxford: Oxford University Press, 1979).

[22]Alan Simpson, *Puritanism in Old and New England* (Chicago: The University of Chicago Press, 1955) 2. Cf. Haller, *Rise of Puritanism* 25.

[23]Ibid., 5.

[24]Ibid., 32-33.

[25]Ibid., 11.

[26]Ibid., 14.

rests on one of the furthest-reaching tenets of the Reformation; the principle of *sola fides*, which removes the center of authority from ecclesiastical institutions and relocates it in the elect soul.[27]

''In this view,'' he continues,

> the norms of the good life were eschatological, not institutional. Behind every experience of the saint stood Jesus Himself, *exemplum exemplorum* for both the believer and the organic body of believers. The way to salvation lay in an internalized, experiential reliving of His life.[28]

Under this schema individuals related more directly to God, and responsibility for their Christian identity and destiny rested more with themselves than with the institutional church.

This enlarged sense of personal responsibility and moral duty also shaped much of Reformed thought, as can be seen in its doctrine of good works. To avoid any possible misunderstanding, Calvin repeatedly insisted that any righteousness which we might claim is not of ourselves but attributed to us by God and only because Christ acquired it for us by His obedience, death and resurrection.[29] But, he noted, ''after we have become sharers in the life of Christ, not only are we ourselves counted as righteous but our works also are reckoned as just in the eyes of God; for what is imperfect in them is covered by the blood of Christ.''[30] Moreover, being engrafted into Christ and enabled by the Holy Spirit, the Christian ought increasingly to grow in willing obedience to the commandments of God. For Calvin sanctification was an inseparable part of justification.[31]

How he envisioned the relationship between good works and assurance of salvation added further incentive for spiritual discipline. According to Steven Ozment, ''Calvin described good works variously as 'testimonies of God's indwelling and ruling in us . . . fruits of the saints' regeneration . . . proofs of the indwelling of the Holy Spirit and signs of the [saints'] calling by which they realize their election.' ''[32] They do not merit salvation, ''yet regular good

---

[27]Bercovitch, *Puritan Origins* 10.

[28]Ibid.

[29]John Calvin, *Institutes of the Christian Religion*, ed. John T. McNeill (Philadelphia: The Westminster Press, 1960) III, i-xix.

[30]Cited in Wilhelm Niesel, *The Theology of Calvin* (Philadelphia: The Westminster Press, 1956) 136.

[31]John Calvin, *Institutes* III, xvi, 1. See also Jaroslav Pelikan, *The Christian Tradition: A History of the Development of Doctrine* (Chicago: The University of Chicago Press, 1984) 4:206.

[32]Steven Ozment, *The Age of Reform, 1250-1550: An Intellectual and Religious History of Late Medieval and Reformation Europe* (New Haven: Yale University Press, 1980) 378.

works are clear signs of present divine favor and assure him [the saint] that
he is on the path to glory.''[33] Consequently, ''religious confidence is . . .
'formed' by the fruits of self-discipline as well as by the promises of God; in
actual practice, good works are presumptive evidence that one is among the
elect.''[34] As a result, more significance was ascribed to good works or moral
conduct. And since persons must participate in these endeavors, this perspective on soteriology further generated some anxiety over the burning
question of whether persons in fact had done enough to be in God's favor.

Puritans experienced these same spiritual dynamics with even greater intensity. In keeping with Reformation teachings on human depravity, they repeatedly and vividly denounced human sinfulness and were quick to deprecate
self-aggrandizement, viewing self as man's greatest enemy.[35] Yet, ironically, precisely because of their preoccupation with deprecating self, they drew
more attention to it and provided more grounds for self-assertion. As Bercovitch explains it:

> The vehemence of the metaphors, the obsessiveness of the theme, the stac-
> cato syntax, the sense of clauses recoiling rather than progressing (since every
> gesture against I-ness contains its own counter-gesture), the interminable-
> because-unresolved incantations of the ''I'' over itself—every aspect of style
> betrays a consuming involvement with ''me'' and ''mine'' that resists dis-
> integration. We cannot help but feel that the Puritans' urge for self-denial
> stems from the subjectivism of their outlook, that their humility is coexten-
> sive with personal assertion.[36]

Paradoxically, their attacks upon self backfired; even the process of self-de-
nial was a provocation of self, leading to greater self-assertion.

That increased self-assertion was partly exercised by assigning an enlarged role to persons in the process of salvation. In keeping with the Reformation principle of justification by faith alone, the Puritans denied that good
works had any meritorious value. Yet they chafed under the unpredictability
and inscrutability of Calvin's God and scrambled valiantly for some alter-
natives.[37] They found one such option in covenant theology, for simply to
place salvation into the context of a covenant implied that persons were obligated to fulfil their terms of the contract. But the Puritans went further. Based

---

[33]Ibid., 378-79.

[34]Ibid., 379.

[35]Bercovitch, *Puritan Origins* 17-18.

[36]Ibid., 18.

[37]Perry Miller, *Errand into the Wilderness*, Harper Torchbooks (New York: Harper &
Row, Publishers, 1956) 53-56.

on covenant thought, they devised an elaborate "doctrine of preparation,"[38] in which they maintained that persons could at least take some preparatory steps to receive God's grace. And forging ahead from that crack in the armor of God's sovereignty, through an ingenious pursuit of covenant logic, some Puritans dared to argue that the anxious soul may even obligate God to grant saving faith.[39] In summary, "It is the fault of man if he does not take the Covenant, and it is his fault again if, having taken it, he does not keep it."[40]

Revising Reformed soteriology from the perspective of covenant theology also enlarged the function of good works. From that view, obedience became a major and indispensable condition of the covenant. Robert Harris ventured to say, God

> hath created vs, called vs, sanctified vs, etc.; and all to obedience. All that God doth by way of mercy or correction, looks this way. The whole creation teacheth obedience, the Bible teacheth it, all diuinity is practicall, and calls for obedience.[41]

Similar exhortations to obedience became one of the most common themes in Puritan sermons and writings. They did not deny that, in the last analysis, God is the efficient cause of our obedience as well as of our faith but obligated persons to share those responsibilities. They stressed practical divinity; theory must be backed by practice. "For all their scholasticism," Bercovitch observed, "the Puritans exalted will above intellect, experience above theory, precept, and tradition."[42]

They did not attribute any salvific value to good works but alleged that regeneration produced fruits of the spirit which are manifested in outward and observable conduct. Being visible, good works became tangible evidence of regeneration and a more reliable basis for assurance of salvation than Calvin was prepared to grant. One's standing with God had become, in a sense, an open book both to oneself and others. This naturally imposed considerable new pressure to perform, in order to prove one's election.

The psychological impact of this view was twofold. On the one hand, it provided welcome relief from the grievous uncertainty created by a God who elected persons to salvation according to His mere pleasure. On the other hand,

---

[38]See Norman Pettit, *The Heart Prepared: Grace and Conversion in Puritan Spiritual Life* (New Haven: Yale University Press, 1966).

[39]Miller, *Errand* 71-82.

[40]Miller, *New England Mind* 394.

[41]Robert Harris, *A Treatise of the New Covenant: Delivered Sermon-Wise Upon, Ezechiel 11, Vers. 19, 20* (London: John Barlet, 1632) 141.

[42]Bercovitch, *Puritan Origins* 21. Cf. John H. Leith, *Assembly at Westminster: Reformed Theology in the Making* (Richmond, Va.: John Knox Press, 1973) 97-99.

it placed a greater onus on individuals to fulfil their conditions in the covenant of grace. Therefore, in a sense, it only replaced the old anxiety over whether God had elected them with a new anxiety over whether they were meeting the conditions of the covenant. Augmented by a generous dose of idealism, absolute moral standards and deadly seriousness, the Puritans became the "most activist of the Reformers."[43] Their obsession to perform was so relentless and compelling that several prominent scholars have assessed it as the single most important dynamic of Puritan religious life.[44]

What has just been described was the context out of which the Baptists emerged, their roots as a movement. It was like the air they breathed and the food they ate. Because these were the burning issues of those days, they were common knowledge and their influence was unavoidable. Further, because the issues were decisive and momentous ones, they were usually adhered to tenaciously.

Is it then possible that Baptists were conceived and nurtured by that Puritan environment but embarked on their own venture from a significantly different point of departure and adopted a fundamentally different operating principle? Were they functioning on a operating system in which ecclesiology rather than soteriology was the key? As the left wing of the Puritan movement, one would more naturally expect the Baptists to have taken that movement's positions to greater extremes rather than to have backed away from them. Or, as sectarians, one would expect them to be more concerned about personal holiness than about church polity. Were Baptists an exception to all of these logical expectations?

If the essence of a movement necessarily corresponds with the quantity of materials its members write on a subject, then Baptists did discard their Puritan heritage. Early Baptists, admittedly, did not write much on soteriological themes; they wrote much more extensively on some other subjects.[45] Other factors, however, must be considered in weighing this issue. Religious liberty, the separation of church and state, believers' churches and believers' baptism were illegal and were extremely volatile subjects in England during the rise and formation of the Baptist movement. So Baptists were under much more pressure to defend those ideas. They were barraged from all sides on these issues, being jostled by other religious groups and repressed by the state. On the other hand, solicitude for more conscientious Christian living was widespread, and the Puritans had produced a literal flood of materials on the

---

[43]Bercovitch, *Puritan Origins* 16.

[44]Most of the interpretations listed in footnote 21, with the possible exception of Schneider and Miller.

[45]See, for example, H. Leon McBeth, *English Baptist Litearture.*

subject before Baptists had the manpower to write anything. Therefore, early Baptists largely drew upon what was already available.[46] In fact, to have duplicated those efforts would have been poor stewardship of time, considering the other battles that needed to be fought. Consequently, Baptists naturally wrote more about their much maligned distinctives, which they alone chose to defend.

Secondly, the essence of a movement does not necessarily lie in its most distinctive characteristic. Distinctiveness is only one connotation of the term essence. Other connotations point to that basic trait or set of traits which define the true substance or intrinsic being of a thing. It is the central tenet, the fundamental conviction or deepest level of spiritual orientation which has shaped the whole. This might be a movement's most distinctive characteristic, but it need not be.

That essence for Baptists lies in their soteriology. Like other Protestants they shifted some responsibility for salvation from the institutional church and its functionaries to the individual. More than other Protestants they took a radical anti-institutional stance, as is represented by their emphasis on soul liberty, individual interpretation of Scripture, the priesthood of all believers, and the autonomy of the local church. The outcome was a church with greatly diminished authority and power and individual believers with greatly increased choice and responsibility. That general anti-institutional stance also carried over to their soteriology, with the result that Baptists shifted responsibility to individuals more radically than Luther, Calvin or the Puritans.

That shift can be seen, for instance, in the role Baptists ascribed to persons in the process of salvation. Particular Baptists closely identified with Puritan theology at this point, although they seem to have made less of covenant theology. As Arminians, the General Baptists, however, made more place for human freedom over against the sovereignty of God, enabling them to go even further in that direction than Puritans utilizing the leverage of covenant theology. Since the seventeenth century numerous other factors have moved Baptists progressively further toward free will until Baptist and free will (including personal responsibility) have come to be considered as practically synonymous.

More particularly, the essence of Baptists lay in an emphasis on sanctification. The progressive shift in emphasis from justification to sanctification which is evidence from Luther to Calvin and the Puritans continued with the Baptists. Thus, the stress upon obedience and practical religious experience which they inherited from the Puritans in itself surpassed that of their Protestant predecessors. Moreover, like the Anabaptists and Puritans, they con-

---

[46]Cf. Hudson, *Baptist Manual*, 21-22.

ceived of the Christian life as a covenant relationship in which both faith and obedience were indispensable and inseparable. One has both or neither. They did not deny justification by faith alone but shifted the emphasis to moral behavior. Good works were viewed as not only an expression of gratitude or a consequence of regeneration but increasingly as part and parcel of salvation.

Part of that shift in focus from justification to sanctification, from the objective to the subjective, also entailed a growing stress on religious experience. Puritans were characterized by an experiential feature "certainly as intense as" that of any other analogous contemporary movement.[47] Baptists, however, shared that experiential thrust, as has been argued elsewhere.[48] For them, too, Christianity was more a way of life than a theology or theory. Repentance, the new birth and sanctification were all to be experienced in a personal and meaningful way and were frequently experienced by them in an intense and profound sense.

What are the historical evidences of these claims? If Baptists shared the Puritan burden for living a devout and holy life, there would surely be some evidence of it. Even though they did not write extensively on the subject, they must at least have indicated concurrence. Such evidence can be found in a variety of sources: confessions of faith, polemical writings, sermons, devotional materials and spiritual autobiographies.[49] Since space does not permit a report from all of these sources, confessions of faith will be singled out and with particular reference to the doctrine of sanctification. They are the most important source of Baptist thought in the seventeenth century, because they were approved by entire associations and, in some cases, by representatives of churches from all of England.

In view of their significance, it is all the more astonishing that the most prominent and widely used Baptist confessions drew so heavily on Puritan counterparts. The authors of the London Confession of 1644, for instance, "borrowed considerably" from the Separatist confession of 1596,[50] and "largely anticipated the Westminster Confession."[51] Finding no defect in the organization of the Westminster and Savoy Confessions and consenting with both "in all the fundamental articles of the Christian religion," the writers of

---

[47]Miller, *New England Mind* 57.

[48]Edwin S. Gaustad, "Baptists and Experimental Religion," *The Chronicle* 15 (July 1952): 110-20; E. Glenn Hinson, "Southern Baptists: A Concern for Experiential Conversion," 137-48.

[49]Sometimes even core values are held unconsciously and are communicated by assumptions and behaviors instead of words.

[50]B. R. White, *Separatist Tradition* 167.

[51]William L. Lumpkin, *Baptist Confessions of Faith* (Chicago: The Judson Press, 1959) 146.

the influential Second London Confession concluded "it best to follow their example, in making use of the very same words with them both, in those articles (which are very many) wherein our faith and doctrine is the same with theirs."[52] Even the Orthodox Creed (1678) of the General Baptists used the Westminster Confession as a model.[53] The General Baptists naturally added some Arminian flavor at appropriate points but showed no less passion about sanctification than the Calvinists. Similarly, Keach's Catechism, the most widely used catechism among Baptists, followed the pattern of the Shorter Catechism of the Westminster divines.

No Baptist confession of faith explicitly identified soteriology, much less sanctification, as its essence. But then one should not expect that; it would be uncharacteristic of a confession of faith to single out a single theme as its essence, and few religious movements label one trait as their core, especially during their formative years. Nevertheless, the space allotted to topics and certain telling statements provide a gage to the thinking of the writers.

Like the Puritan confessions, those of the Baptists gave more space to soteriological subjects than to any others. An examination of the confessions with this focus is quite revealing, especially if one notes articles on the soteriological purposes of God, christological articles on the work of Christ related to salvation, ecclesiastical articles on the soteriological mission of the churches and eschatological articles reflective of soteriological concerns, in addition to the classical soteriological themes. The majority of confessions are largely devoted to this broader range of issues, and some consist almost entirely of them. At the same time, usually only a few articles are utilized for the subjects of the believers' church or believers' baptism, even though Baptists were most distinctive at those points.

More cogent are sporadic but decisive statements in the confessions which seem to reveal the deepest values and aspiration of their authors. Even though they, again, do not directly identify sanctification as the organizing principle of Baptist theology, they do indicate that the authors' underlying convictions and passions lie in this area. In this vein, The Faith and Practice of Thirty Congregations states as its first purpose that it is "to inform those who have a desire to know what *Religious Duties*" Baptists hold forth,[54] and Article 52 declares:

> that the *chief or only* ends of a people baptised according to the counsel of God, when they meet together as the congregation or fellowship of Christ, are, or ought to be, *for to walk sutably [sic]*; or *to give up themselves unto*

---

[52]Ibid., 245.

[53]Ibid., 296.

[54]Ibid., 174.

> *a holy conformity to all the Laws or Ordinances of Jesus Christ*, answerable
> to the gifts and graces received, improving them for the glory of God, and
> the edification of each other in love.[55] (Italics mine.)

Besides noting that Christ is our law-giver, who has given rules to live by
(Article XVIII) and that faith produces conformity to the will, graces and virtues of Christ (Article XXIII), The Somerset Confession (1656) uncharac-
teristically inserted twenty-one specific commandments of Christ, by which
Christians are to glorify God and comfort their souls (Article XXV).[56] Speaking to the necessity of practicing a holy demeanor, The Standard Confession
(1660) reminded its readers that "without holiness no man shall see the Lord"
(Hebrews 12:14).[57] But the strongest emphasis on sanctification comes through
in the most influential Second London Confession (1677). Although essentially a paraphrase of the Westminster Confession, in a preface its Baptist authors declared their confession to be a statement of doctrine "which with our
hearts we most firmly believe, and *sincerely endeavour to conform our lives
to*" and expressed the hope that:

> the *only* care and contention of all upon whom the name of our blessed Re-
> deemer is called, might for the future be, *to walk humbly with their God,*
> and in the exercise of all Love and Meekness towards each other, *to perfect
> holyness in the fear of the Lord,* each one endeavouring to have his conver-
> sation such as becometh the Gospel; and also, suitable to his place and ca-
> pacity, *vigorously to promote in others the practice of true Religion and
> undefiled in the sight of God and our Father.* (Italics mine).[58]

The preface closes on the same note:

> We shall conclude with our earnest prayer, that the God of grace, will pour
> out those measures of his holy Spirit upon us, that the profession of truth
> may be accompanyed with the sound belief, *and diligent practise of it by us*
> (Italics mine); that his name may in all things be glorified, through Jesus
> Christ our Lord, *Amen.*[59]

Although not always that explicit, this deep concern for moral discipline
pervades most early Baptist confessions, even though they are essentially objective statements of Christian doctrines. It was the Baptists' burden that "none
might deceive themselves, by resting in, and trusting to, a form of Godliness,
without the power of it, and inward experience of the efficacy of those truths

---

[55]Ibid., 183.

[56]Ibid., 208-11.

[57]Ibid., 229.

[58]Ibid., 246-47.

[59]Ibid., 248.

that are professed by them.''[60] In any case, there is no evidence of backing away from the Puritan stance; if anything, Baptists intensified it.

If certain soteriological themes then have been adjudged to be the essence of the Puritans, it should be no different for the Baptists? In fact, there are reasons to think that they may even have exceeded the Puritans in this regard. In their writings, Baptists necessarily had to devote more attention to defending their distinctives. But even there the underlying motive was their concern for quality Christian living, as is seen in their concept of a believers' church. As sectarians, they had more reason to stress personal appropriation of religion through an experience of God over against a more passive dependence upon objective grace, dispensed by an institutional church. In addition, their emphasis on complete dependence and consistent obedience to Scripture contributed to a literalistic and legalistic reading of biblical ethics. Like the Anabaptists, they also came to speak of real righteousness over against imputed righteousness: the Christian must acquire personal righteousness and overcome temptations. Forgiveness of sin was viewed as only a part of salvation, which must be accompanied by walking in newness of life. Thus, Baptists were not only committed to discipleship but were zealous in their obedience and preoccupied with moral discipline.

Furthermore, as legally, economically and educationally disadvantaged persons, Baptists naturally exalted religious experience above knowledge and tradition. It was natural for them to emphasize that facet of the Christian life for which they were best qualified. In fact, apart from personal religious experiences, even religious liberty and its various ramifications of a believers' church were considered inconsequential; they had significance only in facilitating a core religious commitment.

Depth of conviction and intensity of experience are two ways to judge the essence of a movement. Another measure is the relationship between the essence and the rest of a movement. The essence serves as the primary source of the rest, as the organizing principle around which the system is built. Deep concern for quality Christian living serves that function well for Baptists. All characteristic Baptist emphases stem from that central hub and can be traced back to it either directly or through other derivatives of it. In fact, they flow from that core naturally, logically and necessarily.

CONCLUSION

For all religious groups some doctrine of salvation is admittedly significant. Among all of them, however, that doctrine is variously understood and/or different components of it are emphasized. For Baptists the focus has been

---

[60]Also in the preface of the Second London Confession. Ibid., 247.

on sanctification, understood primarily as willing and humble obedience to the will of God in thought and action.

Clarity at this point is crucial in understanding the Baptist identity. Viewing an emphasis on quality Christian living as the essence of Baptists is an entree to the movement and an angle of vision which illuminates much about their characteristic thinking, about their distinctive institutional structures and polity, and about their distinguishing ideals and loyalties. Other interpretations of Baptists may not deny this perspective and may even assume it but tend to lose its significance by divergent foci and even lead one to believe that the essence lies elsewhere.

The essence of a movement must not only be acknowledged but nurtured if it is not to be lost. And if lost or abandoned, the result is essentially a different movement. In the case of the Baptists, it follows, we have been playing with the risk of losing our very identity and mission. Baptists, through their distinctive witness, have made enormous contributions to the world and continue to have a mission far too vital to abandon or relinquish.

THE BAPTIST ASSOCIATION IN COLONIAL AMERICA, 1707-1814[1]

WALTER B. SHURDEN
MERCER UNIVERSITY
MACON GA 31207

INTRODUCTION

In 1944 Robert G. Torbet published *A Social History of the Philadelphia Baptist Association*. That particular work contained some of the themes Torbet developed in his later historical writings. These themes were ecumenism, the social nature of the gospel, the Baptist ministry, Baptist missions, and Baptist ecclesiology and thology.

This essay focuses on one of Torbet's life-long concerns: Baptist ecclesiology and its organizational expressions. Specifically, this paper addresses the origin and character of Baptist associations in American prior to the formation of the Triennial Convention in 1814.

THE ENGLISH ROOTS OF ASSOCIATIONS

To understand the chronological development of associations one must turn to England, Ireland, and Wales, for it was there that connectional organizations began among Baptists. Considerable difficulty surrounds the pre-

---

[1]This article is a slightly revised version of W. B. Shurden, "The Historical Background of Baptist Associations," *Review and Expositor* 77 (1980) 161-75.

cise dating and location of the first Baptist association. Part of the difficulty centers on making the distinction of when informal cooperation between churches becomes formal organization.

Informal cooperation among Baptist churches may be dated as early as 1626. In that year five General Baptist churches in the London area joined in communicating with the Waterlander Mennonites of Amsterdam.[2] One of the first instances of such activity among Particular Baptists came in 1644 when seven Particular Baptist churches in London issued a confession of faith. Thirty General Baptist churches in the Midlands cooperated in 1651 by issuing a confession known as *The Faith and Practice of Thirty Congregations*.[3] Interchurch relationships existed, therefore, prior to formal associational structure.

During the 1650s more formal expressions of connectionalism developed with regularly scheduled meetings. Statements of purpose of an association as well as constitutions were eventually adopted. By 1660 "associations had become a typical Baptist institution."[4] Both General and Particular Baptist churches formed associations in the 1650s. However, because the General Baptist pattern of interchurch gatherings had little influence on associationalism in America, attention here will be focused on developments among Particular Baptists in England.

B. R. White has performed a significant service to Baptist historical scholarship by collecting, transcribing, and annotating the records of early Particular Baptist associations which operated during the 1650s. These records, which depict the earliest associations as "General Meetings," reveal much about the earliest patterns of Baptist interchurch relationships as well as the concerns and preoccupations of the individual congregations.[5]

On November 6-7, 1650, three churches of South Wales—Hay, Lanharan, and Ilston—met in what may be called the first Baptist Association. The elders and messengers of the three churches gathered "to consult . . . concerninge such businesses as are, through God's assistance, by them now determined. . . . "[6] The "businesses" dealt with in this General Meeting for the following four years were many and diverse, but the major issues were

---

[2]W. T. Whitley, *A History of British Baptists* (London: Charles Griffin and Company, Limited, 1923) 50.

[3]For the 1644 and 1651 confessions see William L. Lumpkin, *Baptist Confessions of Faith* (rev. ed., Valley Forge, PA: The Judson Press, 1919) 144, 171.

[4]W. T. Whitley, "Association Life till 1815," *Transactions of the Baptist Historical Society*, 5 (January 1916): 24.

[5]See B. R. White, ed. *Association Records of the Particular Baptists of England, Wales, and Ireland to 1660* (London: The Baptist Historical Society, 1971, 1973, 1974).

[6]Ibid., 3.

"the great scarcity" of able ministers and the need for unity between and within the churches. At the fifth General Meeting of these churches the general purpose of the association was spelled out: " . . . the common design was the edification and comfort of the churches."[7] This sounds very similar to the stated intention of the Philadelphia Association, organized in America in 1707. The Philadelphia records state that the churches were to dispatch capable members of their congregations " . . . to meet at the yearly meeting to consult about such things as were wanting in the churches, and to set them in order."[8] So the earliest associational records from Britain and America suggest that the association was made for the churches, not the churches for the association.

If the General Meeting of the churches in South Wales is not designated as the first Baptist association,[9] the honor should go to the Abingdon Association. Messengers from Particular Baptist churches in Abingdon, Reading, and Henley gathered on 8 October 1652, and concluded that "perticular churches of Christ ought to hold a firme communion each with other. . . . "[10] They gave three reasons for the "firme communion." The first was the need for mutual advice and counsel in controversial matters. The second was the need for churches to give and receive in case of financial needs. And the third, more general, was to carry on "the work of God." The messengers also gave considerable attention to the theological basis of the association.

In June 1653, ten Calvinistic Baptist churches of Ireland, who described themselves as "the churches of Christ in Ireland walking together in the faith and order of the Gospell . . . " sent a letter to the Particular Baptist churches of London, urging correspondence and communication between all the Particular Baptist churches of England, Scotland, and Wales. "Let not this sad subject of long sylence be any more amongst us but rather let us be constant provokers of each other to every good word and work by our epistles. . . . "[11] While this Irish letter does not explicitly advocate or necessarily foster associational organizations, it does reflect and strongly encourage a denominational spirit of togetherness. Moreover, it represents the con-

---

[7]Ibid., 8.

[8]A. D. Gillette, editor, *Minutes of the Philadelphia Baptist Association* (Philadelphia: American Baptist Publication Society, 1851) 25.

[9]Available detail records indicate that the last General Meeting of the churches in South Wales was held in August, 1654, or at the latest, 1656. The brevity of this connectional experiment and the absence of formal constitutional documents would cause some to see the South Wales meetings as informal cooperation rather than formal organization. However, the associational model was clearly established in South Wales.

[10]White, *Association Records of . . .* 126.

[11]Ibid., 117.

certed action of the Irish churches. They had "associated" together for the purpose of intensifying denominational awareness.

Associationalism also developed in the west of England. The first of "several general meetings of messengers" from churches in Somerset and adjacent counties occurred in 1653. Documents relating to this association, called the Western or Somerset, reflect two practices which became basic to later associational life in America. These practices were the answering of "queries" and the writing of a circular letter. "Queries" were questions submitted to the General Meeting by individuals or local churches. In answering the "queries," the General Meetings provided what B. R. White described as "a body of case-law for the guidance of their people."[12] Problems represented by the queries ranged from the awesome to the absurd. In 1657 the church at Stoke submitted the following query: "Whether a man in any case in ruling over his wife may lawfully strike her?" The association answered: "He ought so to rule over his wife in wisdom as that the ordinance of God in point of ruling may be preserved and if it may be by any means without striking of her such a proceeding being without any pretext or example that we read of in the holy scripture."[13] Other, and more humane, queries depict troublesome issues for seventeenth century Baptists: the laying on of hands, baptism, the singing of psalms, the doctrine of election, and the nature of the ministry.

In addition to answers to queries, each General Meeting produced a letter to the churches. These letters, often little more than elaborations of issues raised by the queries, provide further insight into the nature of Baptist discipleship and churchmanship in the mid-seventeenth century Associational letters, moreover, exerted a significant shaping power on the discipleship and churchmanship. This associational influence was augmented in 1656 when the association issued "The Somerset Confession of Faith."[14] The Somerset Confession was one of the first in a long history of associational confessions of faith. Calvinistic Baptist associations in America eventually adopted confessional statements as a matter of course.

In the Midlands, organized associational life began in 1655. This General Meeting met thirteen times between 2 May 1655, and 5-6 October 1658. At its first meeting a confession of faith was adopted. The queries presented to this association mirror many of the same problems common to associations in other areas.[15]

---

[12]Ibid., 53.

[13]Ibid., 69.

[14]Lumpkin, *Baptist Confessions* 200-16.

[15]For records of this early association in the Midlands see White, *Association Records of . . .* 18-42.

Baptists in seventeenth century England believed that Christ gave authority to each distinct congregation to direct its own affairs. Such church independence did not obviate, however, the need for some type of cooperation with other independent churches. In fact, Baptists were prohibited from becoming isolationists by practical as well as theological concerns.

Numerous practical factors acted as unifying forces in Baptist life. Four are mentioned here. The first is what Hugh Wamble referred to as "cultic conservation."[16] This was the effort of English Baptists to defend themselves against such external challenges as Quakerism and Fifth Monarchism and the internal dissension regarding such issues as mixed marriages, laying on of hands, and hymn-singing. In associating together Baptist churches both established and preserved a Baptist tradition.

A second practical factor which brought independent Baptist churches together was the need for fellowship. Baptists were a harassed minority in seventeenth century England and therefore needed the encouragement and strength afforded by associational meetings.[17] Evangelism was a third cause, as well as objective, of early English Baptist associationalism. Confessions of faith issued by Baptist associations served not only purposes of apologetics, but also of evangelism. Statements from Baptists acting jointly both clarified and perpetuated their point of view.

Scattered congregations belonging to the same church was the fourth factor which encouraged the development of the Baptist association. Because of distance and lack of ministers, rural churches, especially, would be divided into several congregations which came together periodically for discipline and communion. After becoming distinct churches, the scattered congregations maintained their fraternal relationship. Such a relationship often developed into organized associational life.[18]

Theologically, the seventeenth century Baptist concept of the church facilitated the progress of interchurch connectionalism. The Baptist interpretation of the relationship of the universal or invisible church to the local or visible church provided the doctrinal justification for the association. Believing that the local church was related to the universal church as a part to the whole, Baptists could permit the parts, the local churches, to relate to each in some connectional form.[19]

---

[16]Hugh Wamble, "The Concept and Practice of Christian Fellowship: The Connectional and Inter-denominational Aspects Thereof, Among Seventeenth Century English Baptists" (Th.D. diss., Southern Baptist Theological Seminary, Louisville, Kentucky, 1955) 314-17.

[17]Ibid., 313.

[18]Ibid., 255-74.

[19]Ibid., 547ff.

The confession of faith issued by the seven Particular Baptist churches in London, while carefully safeguarding local church independence, gave explicit approval of churches associating together. Article XLVII of the confession declared:

> And although the particular Congregations be distinct and severall Bodies, every one a compact and knit citie in it self; yet are they all to walk by one and the same Rule, and by all means convenient to have the counsell and help one of another in all needfull affaires of the church, as members of one body in the common faith under Christ their onely head.[20]

Early associational records make it clear that Baptists considered individual churches to be members of the one church of Jesus Christ. At the second General Meeting of the churches in the Midlands, the messengers of those churches affirmed:

> . . . we do, therefore, according to the will of God, clearly appearing in his word, with true thankfullnes unto him for his grace, mutually acknowledge each other to be true churches of Christ, and that it is our duty to hold a close communion each to the other as the Lord shall give opportunity and ability. . . .[21]

These churches also covenanted to be mutually helpful ''in watching over each other and considering each other for good in respect of puritie of doctrine, exercise of love and good conversation'' because they considered the churches to be ''all members of the same body of Christ.''[22]

Probably the clearest and most sophisticated statement of the theological basis for associationalism came from the Abingdon Association. At the organizational meeting in 1652, the Abingdon messengers affirmed that inter-church relationships were necessary ''because there is the same relation betwixt the perticular churches each towards other as there is betwixt perticular members of one church.'' Elaborating upon that principle, the messengers stated:

> For the churches of Christ doe all make up one body or church in general under Christ their head as Eph. 1.22f; Col. 1.24; Eph. 5.23ff; 2 Cor. 12.13f. As perticular members make up one perticular church under the same head, Christ, and all the perticular assemblys are but one Mount Syon, Is. 4.5; Song. 6.9. Christ his undefiled is but one and in his body there is to be no schisme which is then found in body when all the members have not the same care one over another. Wherefore all conclude that every church ought to manifest its care over other churches as fellow members of the same body

---

[20]Lumpkin, *Baptist Confessions* 168, 169.

[21]White, *Association Records of . . .* 20.

[22]Ibid., 21.

of Christ in general do rejoice and mourne with them, according to the law of their mere relation in Christ.[23]

When Baptist associations developed in America, they followed, for the most part, the patterns developed by Particular Baptists in England. They were organized in much the same way and for the same reasons. They justified their existence in the same way. They answered queries, wrote circular letters, dealt with local church squabbles, all reminiscent of the English Particular Baptist pattern. And like the English associations, associations in America protected local church independency while advocating connectionalism.

ASSOCIATIONAL MODELS IN COLONIAL AMERICA

From their inception in seventeenth century England, Baptists contained within their denominational family several different groups with varying emphases. Characterized by a different theological interpretation of the atonement, the two earliest and most significant groups were the Particular and the General Baptists. Particular Baptists followed the teaching of John Calvin and affirmed a ''particular'' or ''limited'' atonement, available only for the elect. General Baptists, on the other hand, believed the atonement to be of a ''general'' nature and accessible to all. Transplanted in America by immigration, these two groups, plus an indigenous American movement known as the Separate Baptists, comprised most of the Baptist life and action in colonial America.

The Particular Baptists

So as to distinguish themselves from the Separate Baptists, Particular Baptists eventually became known as Regular Baptists in America. The terms ''Particular'' and ''Regular'' will be used interchangeably in this article. Among the Particular Baptists the Philadelphia Association was the first and, by far, most important Baptist body of its kind in America. Henry C. Vedder believed that by adopting a strongly Calvinistic confession of faith in 1742 the association ''fixed the character of the denomination for all time.''[24] The association was prominent enough in its influence on later associations that historians have come to refer to ''the Philadelphia tradition.''[25]

---

[23]Ibid., 126. For two articles on English Baptist associations see B. R. White, ''The Organisation of the Particular Baptists, 1644-1660,'' *The Journal of Ecclesiastical History* 17 (October 1966): 209-26; and R. Dwayne Conner, ''Early English Baptist Associations,'' *Foundations* 15 (April-June 1972): 163-85.

[24]Henry C. Vedder, *A History of the Baptists in the Middle States* (Philadelphia: American Baptist Publication Society, 1898) 92.

[25]See Winthrop S. Hudson, ed. *Baptist Concepts of the Church* (Chicago: The Judson Press, 1959) 30.

Imitating its English Particular Baptist forerunners as to doctrine polity, and essential structure, the Philadelphia Association became the point of orientation for most American associations. Early important associations like the Charleston, Ketocton, and Kehukee in the South, the Warren in the East, and the Elkhorn and Salem on the frontier of Kentucky reflected and perpetuated the essential pattern established by Philadelphia.

The dominance of Regular Baptist associational polity may be accounted for in several ways. Besides being the first association, the Philadelphia organization had the added advantage of being centrally located and in the area of Baptists' earliest numerical strength. Moreover, the association claimed some of the most competent leadership in colonial America. These leaders preached the advantages of associationalism as they itinerated throughout the country. Oliver Hart initiated the first association in the South, while James Manning was responsible for the first Particular Baptist association in the East. Both men were nurtured in the Philadelphia tradition. Also, because of the relative insignificance of General Baptists in America and the later merger of Separate Baptists with the Regulars, the Philadelphia pattern eventually prevailed. The theological climate produced by the Great Awakening also gave the Calvinistically oriented Philadelphians a firmer grip on the American Baptist future.

Concerned initially with a desire for fellowship, communication between the churches, and ministerial discipline, Regular Baptists eventually used their associations as the denominational voice for missions, education, and religious liberty. Associationalism also created a denominational solidarity among Baptists in the eighteenth century. By working through associations, Regular Baptists stimulated a Baptist denominational consciousness in colonial America.[26]

Emergency situations often altered associational polity, but usually Regular Baptists thought of associations as autonomous organizations functioning in an advisory role. The term "advisory" could be misleading, however. Baptist associations were not timid counselors, hiding on the fringe of denominational life. Associational "advice" had muscle in it. Local churches and individual Baptists, especially ministers, were cautious of spurning associational suggestions.

In 1749 the Philadelphia Association endorsed an essay written by Benjamin Griffith on the power and authority of an association. Declaring that an association was never meant to be considered "a superior judicature . . . having . . . superintendency over the churches," Griffith nevertheless be-

---

[26]For material in this section see Walter B. Shurden, "Associationalism Among Baptists in America, 1707-1814" (Th. D. diss., New Orleans Baptist Theological Seminary, New Orleans, LA, 1967).

lieved that delegates from the churches, convened in an associated capacity, had "a very considerable power in their hands." The power of which Griffith wrote was the association's power "to exclude the delegates of a defective and disorderly church from an Association, and to refuse their presence at their consultations, and to advise all the churches in confederation to do so."[27] Most definitions of associational authority agreed with Griffith's explication of the power of an association. Yet extensive study in associational documents is not required for one to be convinced that Baptists were far more interested in the freedom and independence of the local church than in extending the powers of the associated body. Most associational constitutions consumed more space indicating what an association could not do than clearly stating what it could do.[28]

What did the Regular Baptist pattern of associationalism give to Baptist life in America? First, it provided the first model of interchurch confederation which injected organization into denominational life. Second, it gave ministerial orderliness and uniformity to the Baptist ministry and local church life. Third, it guaranteed a church polity which honored congregationalism without encouraging isolationism or presbyterianism. Fourth, it established a denominational channel through which Baptist churches could minister in areas of education, missions, and religious liberty.

The General Baptists

In the late seventeenth or early eighteenth century the General Baptists began holding meetings in Rhode Island where churches would send their representatives. These general meetings were referred to interchangeably as quarterly or yearly meetings. The exact date of the initial quarterly meeting is obscure, but John Comer described the June 1729, meeting as the "largest yt (that) ever hath been."[29] Obviously the meeting had been going on for several years.

General Baptist historian Richard Knight said that the meetings began soon after the formation of a few of the first churches in Rhode Island, or about the close of the seventeenth century.[30] Later historians have assigned various dates

---

[27]Benjamin Griffith, "Essay" in Gillette, *Minutes of* . . . 60-62.

[28]For elaboration on associational theory and the bases upon which colonial Baptists justified associations see Shurden, "Associationalism Among . . ." 69-154. A distillation of this material may be seen in two articles by Shurden, "The Associational Principle, 1707-1814: Its Rationale," *Foundations* 21 (July-September 1978), 211-24 and "Church and Association: A Search For Boundaries," *Baptist History and Heritage* 24 (July 1979): 32-40, 61.

[29]John Comer, *The Diary of John Comer*, ed. C. Edwin Barrows (Philadelphia: American Baptists Publication Society, 1892) 66.

[30]Richard Knight, *History of the General or Six Principle Baptists* (Providence, Smith and Parmenter, 1827) 322. Knight actually said "sixteenth century." He obviously meant seventeenth.

to the meeting. One point of general agreement is that the Rhode Island meeting constituted American Baptists' earliest experience in interchurch relationships. Whether or not it should be designated the first Baptist association in America is another question. Very likely, the Rhode Island yearly meeting operated for several years on an informal basis similar to some quarterly meetings which preceded the Philadelphia Association. By 1729 the Rhode Island meeting had assumed the characteristics of a formally organized association. For this reason the General Baptist Yearly Meeting of Rhode Island should definitely be considered the second, if not first, association in America.

Baptist historians have generally ignored this Rhode Island association. Doubtless this is due to the scanty records available for a study of the organization and the historians' interest to look extensively at the much more influential Philadelphia Association. The combination of these Rhode Island churches suggests, however, that it was very similar to the Philadelphia Association in both purpose and activity. The elders and messengers from the churches convened in the Yearly Meeting

> for the strengthening, edifying and upbuilding of each other in the Redeemer's kingdom; in setting in order the things that were wanting; and in advising and assisting in accomodating any difficulties that might arise.[31]

The threefold purpose was fellowship, discipline, and advice, and therefore not unlike associational objectives of the Particular Baptists.

General Baptists never became a dominant force in American Baptist life, and they were almost totally without influence among Southern Baptists. The decline of General Baptists in America is not extremely difficult to explain. Following the Great Awakening, the Calvinistic Baptist churches gained in numerical strength while the General Baptists, whose theology was antithetical to Calvinistic revivalism, suffered reversals. Several early General Baptist churches became extinct. Others changed their theological sentiments and became Calvinists. Also, a scarcity of ministerial leadership was never reinforced by English immigration. With the decline of General Baptists, the more aggressive Particular Baptists gained in influence and power. So while General Baptists were among the first to establish associational life in colonial America, they never exerted a formative influence on Baptist church polity in this country.

The Separate Baptists

The third group of Baptists to constitute associations in America were Separate Baptists. They originated from New England Congregationalism during the Great Awakening. Disturbed by the sterile formalism, unregener-

---

[31]Ibid.

ate church membership, and elevated ministerial authority present in their denomination, some revivalistic Congregationalists withdrew to form new churches which, by their standards, more nearly approximated the New Testament model. These discontented Congregationalists and their churches were dubbed variously as "New Lights," "Separates," and "Strict Congregationalists." The last of these descriptions is significant for Separate Baptist church polity in general and their associational theory in particular. After accepting the cardinal Baptist tenet of believers' baptism, the "Separates" were gradually transformed into the "Separate Baptists."

Under the leadership of Shubal Stearnes a small group of Separate Baptists settled in 1755 at Sandy Creek, North Carolina. Three years later in 1758, they organized the Sandy Creek Baptist Association. For thirteen years Sandy Creek was the only Separate Baptist Association in the south.[32] A dispute in 1770 over associational authority divided the association into three geographical divisions; the Congaree in South Carolina, the General Association of Separate Baptists in Virginia, and the Sandy Creek in North Carolina. Because of the union with the Regular Baptists beginning in 1767, the number of associations composed entirely of Separate Baptists never exceeded ten.

Some historians have suggested that Separate Baptist associational theory initiated a process of centralization in Baptist ecclesiology which was perpetuated in the structure of the Southern Baptist Convention. These interpreters contend that Separate Baptists were profoundly influenced by their semi-presbyterian background. Usually, however, the attempt to identify the Separate Baptists with a centralized ecclesiology is based on the undemocratic activities of the Sandy Creek Association.

The above interpretation should be questioned. For one thing, Separate Baptists of the South, like their New England kinsmen, were radical individualists. This individualism was expressed in their theology, church-state philosophy, and ecclesiology. Rather than duplicating their ecclesiological past, Separate Baptists reacted against it. Moreover, one should not conclude that the Sandy Creek Association, the first Separate Baptist association, articulated what became typical Separate Baptist associational theory. The fact is that Separate Baptists repudiated the view of Shubal Stearnes which permitted the transfer of church power to the association.[33]

It is significant that at the initial meeting of the first Separate Baptist association in Virginia the delegates agreed unanimously that the organization

---

[32]For the possibility of a Separate Baptist association organized in New England in the 1750s or 1760s see William G. McLoughlin, "The First Calvinistic Baptist Association in New England, 1754?-1767," *Church History*, 36 (December 1967): 410-18.

[33]See Morgan Edwards, "Materials towards a History of the Baptists in the Province of North Carolina," 1772, 33.

had "no power or authority to impose anything upon the churches."[34] And Morgan Edwards claimed that the Separate Baptist association in South Carolina had the same "plan, sentiments, and proceedings" as the Philadelphia, not the Sandy Creek Association.[35] Concerning Sandy Creek, any excessive authority manifested in the life of that association should be understood in the light of Shubal Stearnes' patriarchal influence and not as normative Separate Baptist procedure.

The unique feature about Separate Baptist associationalism was not the centralization of authority but the style of the annual meetings. After attending the second meeting of the Sandy Creek Association John Gano, a Regular Baptist, accused the Separate Baptists of being "rather immethodical."[36] Every decision of the association required a unanimous vote! While some business was transacted, the greater emphasis was upon preaching, evangelism, and fellowship. Separate Baptist associational meetings were strikingly similar to the revivalistic camp meetings which developed later on the Kentucky frontier.

The Separate Baptist model of associational life, at least in the early stages of 1758-1800, differed from the Regular Baptists. Regular Baptists came to do business and have fellowship. Separate Baptists came to hear good preaching and that was their fellowship.[37] Both Separates and Regulars contributed, therefore, to the emerging character of associational life. Each modified the other's perception of what an association should be and do. The blending was healthy. The result was a strong and useful connectionalism throughout the first half of the nineteenth century.

THE SPREAD OF ASSOCIATIONS IN AMERICA

Difficulties Prior to 1780

After a full century of activity in colonial America, Baptists had organized only two associations. By 1760 the number had increased to four; by 1770, seven; and by 1780, thirteen. These statistics have been interpreted to mean that associational life developed slowly among Baptists in America. The

---

[34]Robert B. Semple, *A History of the Rise and Progress of the Baptists in Virginia*, revised and extended by B. W. Beale (Richmond: Pitt and Dickinson, 1894) 71.

[35]Morgan Edwards, "Materials towards a History of the Baptists in the Province of South Carolina," 1772, 73.

[36]Semple, *Baptits in Virginia* 66.

[37]For further discussion on Separate Baptist associationalism see James Owen Renault, "The Development of Separate Baptist Ecclesiology in the South," (Ph.D. diss., Southern Baptist Theological Seminary, Louisville, KY, 1978).

reason attributed to this slow development was the Baptist stress on local church independency and the corresponding fear of extra-local ecclesiastical organizations. What appears to be hesitant expansion, however, can be explained by factors other than a radical congregational ecclesiology. In fact, circumstances considered, it may be argued that associational growth among Baptists was not retarded to any great extent.

At least three factors, other than sensitivity to localism, obstructed interchurch connectionalism among Baptists in America prior to the Revolutionary War. Those factors were: (1) lack of numerical strength and ministerial leadership, (2) geographical isolation of the churches, and (3) theological diversity.

Baptists were numerically weak in Colonial America, particularly prior to the Great Awakening. By 1660 only four small Baptist churches had been established in this country. At the turn of the century there were slightly over twenty. But of those, the Calvinistic churches in the Pennsylvania-Jersey region already enjoyed a close, although unorganized, relationship. In his famous "Century Sermon" Samuel Jones said that the beginning of the Philadelphia Association "might with but little impropriety" be extended back "some years" beyond 1707.[38] Likewise, General Baptists of Rhode Island and Massachusetts, as we have already seen, had an informal connectionalism possibly as early as the late seventeenth century. Considering, therefore, their small number and the fact that some semblance of interchurch cooperation existed by 1700, Baptists were not cautious at all in this regard. Moreover, previous contact with associations in Britain would have prepared immigrating Baptists for organizational development in America.

Winthrop Hudson has observed correctly that Baptists did not wait for the multiplication of their churches before forming associations.[39] The Philadelphia Association began with only five churches; the Charleston in 1751 had four, and Sandy Creek in 1758 had three. Meeting in 1765, the only four Regular Baptist churches in Virginia constituted the Ketocton Association. Prior to that they were related to the Philadelphia Association, in addition to holding their own yearly meetings.[40]

Compounding the problem of early associational development was the geographical isolation of the churches. For years Baptist churches outside New England and the Philadelphia area were prohibited by distance from any interchurch relations. The vast territory included in the earliest associations re-

---

[38]Samuel Jones, "A Century sermon," in Gillette, *Minutes of Philadelphia* 454.

[39]Winthrop S. Hudson, "The Associational Principle Among Baptists," *Foundations*, 1 (January 1958): 11.

[40]Semple, *Baptists in Virginia* 388.

veals the difficulties. At one time the Philadelphia Association encompassed churches from New York to Virginia. When the Kehukee Association began in 1765, it included churches from Norfolk, Virginia to Raleigh, North Carolina.[41] And for some time the Warren Association included churches in Rhode Island, Massachusetts, New Hampshire, Vermont, and Connecticut.[42]

The theological diversity among Baptists also created an obstruction in the path of interchurch relationships. Besides the basic theological cleavage which divided the denomination into General Baptists and Particular Baptists, there were Keithian, German, Seventh Day and Separate Baptists. An obvious fact about the early associations is that they were theologically, rather than geographically, constructed. Churches joined associations for reasons of theological affinity and not geographical proximity. Where distance and number of churches permitted, Baptists of kindred minds organized associations soon.[43]

To be sure, some individual Baptists had apprehensions about the nature and power of associational bodies. Isaac Backus is usually remembered as the prime example here. But McLoughlin has demonstrated that Backus had at least some interest in interchurch conferences even prior to this refusal, in 1767, to unite with the Warren Association.[44] Moreover, by 1770 Backus and his church were members of the Warren. While some few, therefore, approached the organization of associations with some reserve, no widespread or deep-rooted prejudice existed on this matter. Suspicion regarding associations was not a major obstacle in the development of Baptist associations in America.

Associational Expansion Following 1780

From 1780 to 1814 Baptists in America organized at least one association per year. Though some of the difficulties hampering associational development continued past 1780, the associational idea had become a permanent fixture of Baptist polity. Between 1780 and 1790 twenty-three new associations were begun, almost twice as many as had been established in the previous one hundred forty years of Baptist life. By 1800 Baptists had forty-eight associations, and by the time of the organizational meeting of the Triennial Convention in 1814, they had one hundred twenty-five. The explanation of this significant expansion is found in the following three factors: (1) the nu-

---

[41]Woodrow Castelloe, "The Kehukee Baptist Association, North Caroline," *The Chronicle* 3 (October 1940): 165.

[42]David Benedict, *A General History of the Baptist Denomination in America* (Boston: Lincoln and Edmands, 1813) 2:509.

[43]For documentation see Shurden, "Associationalism Among . . . , " 34, 35.

[44]McLoughlin, "The First Calvinistic Baptist Association," 412, 413.

merical increase of Baptists, (2) denominational consolidation, and (3) proven associational effectiveness.

At the signing of the Declaration of Independence, Baptists were about one to two hundred sixty-four of the American population. Fourteen years later, in 1800, they were one to fifty-three. Revivalism was primarily responsible for this incredible multiplication. As a result of the Great Awakening, Separate Baptists appeared on the denominational horizon. They injected an evangelistic enthusiasm into the Baptist family which pervaded the entire denomination. Baptists enjoyed additional gains when the Second Great Awakening erupted around the turn of the nineteenth century.

Another development which aided Baptist growth was their devout patriotism to the colonial cause during the Revolutionary War. Before 1776 Baptists were often regarded as "an ignorant illiterate set—and of the poor and contemptible class of people."[45] But their patriotism during the war helped to dislodge prevailing social stigmas. Moreover, persons of prominence joined Baptist churches[46] and a newly acquired religious freedom afforded Baptists new opportunities to present their distinctive witness.[47]

After the revolution Baptists displayed ability to adapt to the frontier and a westward moving population. William Warren Sweet demonstrated that no group was better equipped sociologically, theologically, or ecclesiologically to capture the frontier people than Baptists.[48] The trans-Appalachian frontier accounted for much of the Baptist increase in the first half of the nineteenth century.

Thus, Baptists grew in number because of revivalism, a transformed social image, and their unique adaptability to a new environment. From the increase in individual membership came a corresponding multiplication of the churches, and with the multiplication of the churches came a natural increase in associations. This growth alleviated two problems blocking earlier associational expansion; namely, the numerical deficiency and the geographical isolation of the churches.

The consolidation of divergent Baptist groups in the last half of the eighteenth century also aided associational growth. Many of the older General Baptist churches were transformed into Calvinistic churches in the wake of the Great Awakening. And Separate Baptists and Regular Baptists began a

---

[45]William Fristoe, *A Concise History of the Ketocton Baptist Association* (Staunton, Virginia: William Gilman Lyford, 1808) 64.

[46]Semple, *Baptists in Virginia* 59.

[47]Gillette, *Minutes* 362.

[48]William Warren Sweet, *Religion in the Development of American Culture, 1765-1840* (New York: Charles Scribner's Sons, 1952) 110-14.

gradual process of denominational unification in the 1760s. They merged in New England in 1767, in North Carolina in 1777, in Virginia in 1787, and in Kentucky in 1801.

A common struggle against religious intolerance, a mutual interest in revivalism, and a theological synthesis, based upon the Philadelphia Confession of 1742, facilitated the union. By 1800 most of the Regulars and Separates were working together and cooperating through associations.

A third explanation for the increase of associations was their proven value. Any fear of illegitimate power was dispelled as associations demonstrated concern for protecting rather than usurping the rights of local churches. Associations proved helpful in securing religious liberty, extirpating doctrinal deviations, affording preaching for churches without ministers, encouraging the ministry, and rallying the denomination to the causes of education and missions. Several years after reluctantly joining the Warren Association, Isaac Backus wrote that "the benefits of the Warren Association soon became so evident, that others were formed in many parts of the country."[49] After the associations proved helpful, many associations, like the Mississippi, spoke of the "necessity of a combination of churches."

---

[49]Isaac Backus, *A History of New England*, second edition with notes by David Weston (Newton, Massachusetts: The Backus Historical Society, 1871) 2:410.

THE *BAPTISM, EUCHARIST AND MINISTRY* DOCUMENT: AN OUTLINE OF ONE BAPTIST REFLECTION

DAVID M. SCHOLER
NORTHERN BAPTIST THEOLOGICAL SEMINARY
LOMBARD, IL 60148

This brief outline is my attempt to summarize a discussion of the World Council of Churches' *Baptism, Eucharist and Ministry* document (Faith and Order Paper No. 111; 1982) carried on by the Faculty of Northern Baptist Theological Seminary on 3 October 1985. The context of the discussion was part of the institution's own process of attempting to define Baptist identity.

1. On the document as a whole:

    (1) We commend the ecumenical effort to express shared understandings of faith and practice and believe that such efforts are important for Baptists and their understanding of themselves as part of the Church of the Lord Jesus Christ.

    (2) We are concerned about the following aspects of the *BEM* document:

(a) The Baptist experience/tradition, without denying its continuity with the apostolic traditions of the whole Church, historically and culturally involves conflict and struggle and even a sense of being overagainst the Church-society linkage represented in the dominant orthodox traditions. This experience/tradition shapes a somewhat different understanding or definition of the Church than that often presupposed in the document. This experience/tradition also brings a different perspective to theologizing than that usually reflected or assumed in this document. The document tends to presuppose a rather traditional and institutional Christianity, often with a concern for maintenance, which excludes something of the Baptist emphasis on the meaning of the Church and, therefore, tends to exclude the new, late twentieth century expressions of the Church such as the Latin American base communities or the house churches of China.

(b) The Baptist commitments to individual competency (''soul liberty''), the priesthood of every believer and church autonomy mean that we are concerned that Friends (Quakers) and the Salvation Army (for examples) are Christian traditions whose differences do not receive explicit mention in the text of *BEM*.

(c) There seems to be an inconsistency about what is placed in the text and what is placed in the official commentary. For examples of each, note the following: (1) The last paragraph of Ministry section 18 is purely descriptive and is not a theological affirmation. This paragraph should have been placed outside the text. (2) On the other hand, the first sentence of the commentary in Ministry section 17 is an important finding about the witness of Scripture on the ministry. The Baptist concern for Scripture, not to mention that of the whole Church, would urge that this statement be part of the text.

2. On baptism:
  (1) We commend the following emphases of the Baptism section of *BEM*:
      (a) The stress on the act and action of God in baptism. This is a salutory balance to the traditional Baptist stress on the individual's response and faith toward baptism.
      (b) The emphasis on baptism as an act which involves the whole community overagainst a Baptist tendency to privatize religious acts.
      (c) The many recognitions within the Baptism section (more here than in either the Eucharist or Ministry sections) of the traditions and convictions of Baptists regarding the theology and practice of baptism.

(2) We are concerned about the following aspects of the Baptism section:

(a) Although Baptists have learned to accept others in Christ who practice infant baptism, the emphasis on infant baptism touches Baptists at a crucial theological and historical-cultural point of its self-understanding. Not only do Baptists reject infant baptism on the basis of their theological understanding of the teaching of Scripture, Baptists also rejected infant baptism historically in order to "cut the link" between Church and State which violated the Baptist understanding of the Church (see 1.2) (1) above).

(b) The most objectionable statement in the whole section for Baptists (perhaps in the whole document) is the second sentence of section 13: "Any practice which might be interpreted as 'rebaptism' must be avoided." The absoluteness of "any," "must" and "might be interpreted" are especially offensive to and unacceptable to the majority of Baptists and Baptist tradition.

(c) The Baptist perception of the relationship between faith and baptism is acknowledged (for example in the third sentence of section 8), but is usually not explicitly or clearly enough indicated throughout the section for a Baptist perspective. For example, the first two sentences of section 2 do not mention faith explicitly which, from a Baptist perspective, tends to skew the understanding of baptism. Although the first sentence of section 5 acknowledges that the Holy Spirit works in persons before baptism, the first two sentences of section 7 could appear insensitive to this and could be seen by some Baptists as making baptism prior to the reception of the Spirit. The point is that the language of faith, Spirit and baptism should have greater clarity in the document from a Baptist perspective.

3. On eucharist:

(1) We commend the emphases of the text on the richness present in the Church's understanding of the eucharist. There is much here that Baptists have neglected or ignored that should be used to enrich Baptist understandings and practice with reference to the eucharist. Baptist relfection on the eucharist has tended to be somewhat superficial and shallow.

(2) We are concerned about the following aspects of the Eucharist section:

(a) The emphasis in section 29 on the importance of an ordained minister presiding at the eucharist is too strong for the Baptist tradition. The statement here is even stronger than the one concerning the participation of ordained ministers in baptism (Baptism, section 22), but should not be. Although Baptists today in many parts of the world do emphasize the role of ordained ministers in baptism and the eucharist, the Baptist tradition and much Baptist practice argue against the role for the ordained ministers indicated here in the Eucharist section.

(b) The statement in section 31 that the celebration of the eucharist " . . . should take place at least every Sunday" is too strong for most Baptists. It appears to be dictating a majority practice without proper expression of differences (which is more characteristic in the Baptism section).

4. On ministry:
   (1) We commend the place given to "The Calling of the Whole People of God" in this section.
   (2) We are concerned about the following aspects of the Ministry section:
      (a) The section as a whole simply does not give adequate attention to the importance and roles of the laity in the ministry of the Church; the document in general and throughout is too much concerned with the ordained ministry. Specifically, further, the third sentence of section 12, for example, tends to violate the priesthood of all believers. A Baptist perspective could say "that the whole cmmunity gathered is a reminder of the divine initiative." Again, section 13 should, from a Baptist perspective, specifically note that one of the chief responsibilities of ordained ministers is to equip the whole people of God for their ministries.
      (b) The ministry of women and the inclusion of women in the ordained ministry hardly receives adequate emphasis from our perspective (which represents many, but not all, Baptists). It has been already noted (1,2) (3) (1) that section 18 is a piece of contemporary description. What is needed is a theological affirmation of the inclusion of all persons in the ordained ministry. The document appears to be very cautious on the differences among churches on the ordination of women (see section 54). One wonders why there is such a strong, unyielding statement in the second sentence in Baptism, section 13 (which Baptists cannot accept), but such an open concession to differences on the inclusion of women in God's ministry here?

(c) The emphasis on ministry throughout this section is too maintenance oriented. The statements concerning ministry here are almost devoid of (1) a mission sense; (2) a prophetic sense; and (3)
a recognition of ministry ''outside'' the institutional Church (both
in para-church groups and even in the world). This concern here
is very closely related to the first general concern noted (see 1.2)
(a)).

All of these comments are expressions of one specific group of theological scholars associated with a Baptist graduate theological seminary. The
concern throughout is to encourage and to engage in gracious, open and serious theological dialog and critique, reflecting our ecumenical commitment
to the one Church of the Lord Jesus Christ and our sense of integrity with
reference to our Baptist commitment.